Online!

**The Internet Guide for
Students and Writers**

"Online!"

The Internet Guide for
Students and Writers

Andrew Harnack
and
Eugene Kleppinger

St. Martin's Griffin
New York

Manufactured in the United States of America.

Publisher: Marilyn Moller
Development editor: Talvi Laev
Managing editor: Patricia Mansfield Phelan
Project editor: Harold Chester
Production supervisors: Dennis Para, Kurt Nelson
Design coordinator: Patricia McFadden
Art director: Lucy Krikorian
Text design: Anna George
Trade jacket design: Henry Sene Yee
Trade editor: Corin See

Library of Congress Cataloging-in-Publication Data

Harnack, Andrew.
    Online! : The Internet Guide for Students and Writers / Andrew
Harnack and Eugene Kleppinger.
        p.   cm.
    ISBN 0-312-17094-7
    1. Internet (Computer network)   2. Web sites.   3. Authors—
Computer network resources.   I. Kleppinger, Gene.
TK5105.875.I57H365   1997
025.04—dc21   97-5254
                                                                    CIP

First published in the United States of America by St. Martin's Press

First St. Martin's Griffin Edition: September 1997

10   9   8   7   6   5   4   3   2   1

For information, write to:
St. Martin's Press, Inc.
175 Fifth Avenue
New York, N.Y. 10010

Acknowledgments

"Rules for Breaking URLs," from *Wired Style: Principles of English
Usage in the Digital Age,* edited by Constance Hale. *HardWired,*
1996. Copyright © 1996 by *HardWired.* Reproduced with
permission.

Project Gutenberg homepage. Michael S. Hart, Executive
Director of Project Gutenberg. Reproduced with permission.

Memory Made Manifest: The United States Holocaust Memorial
Museum. Photo courtesy of The United States Holocaust
Memorial Museum and plans for the second through fifth
floors courtesy of Pei Cobb Freed & Partners Architects, New
York, N.Y.

"Meldrum   Family   Genealogy"   by   Ron   Meldrum
<http://www.bates.edu/nmeldrum>.   Reproduced   with
permission.

Contents

Preface

Online! aims to be a useful writer's companion to the Internet, one that offers the help students and teachers have been asking for:

- Help for accessing and evaluating Internet sources
- Models for citing and documenting Internet sources in the MLA, APA, CBE, and *Chicago* styles
- Tips for communicating and publishing on the Internet and the World Wide Web
- Advice on designing a homepage
- A directory of Internet sources in the major academic disciplines

This book was born in early 1996 when we found ourselves unable to provide good answers to our students' questions about citing and documenting Internet sources. Determined to find answers, we read everything we could find on using the Internet for research purposes. We examined every documentation style sheet and manual we could find. Among the several style sheets published on the Internet, we especially admired Janice Walker's "MLA-Style Citations for Electronic Sources" (Version 1.0), first available in February 1996 at <http://www.cas.usf.edu/english/walker/mla.html>. As the first to offer help with Internet source citation, Walker deserves everyone's accolades. All of us who work and teach online owe her an enormous debt of gratitude. But as we worked with her original eight models with our students, even Walker's models seemed to leave some questions unanswered. And so we rolled up our sleeves and went to work. The result is *Online! A Reference Guide to Using Internet Sources.*

After drafting a set of MLA-style guidelines for citing Internet sources and presenting them at several professional conferences in Kentucky, we published "Beyond the *MLA Handbook*: Documenting Electronic Sources on the Internet" in *Kairos: A Journal for Teaching Writing in Webbed Environments* 1.2 (1996) at <http://eng.ttu.edu/kairos/1.2/inbox/mla.html>. That essay identified four areas of citation practice needing improvement and offered an MLA-style guide for distribution to students and researchers. Within days, our email boxes were flooded with requests for permission to reprint and distribute our work, and we have been gratified by the number of teachers, students, librarians, researchers, composition specialists, webmasters, techno-rhetoricians, journalists, and ordinary folk who have written to say that our style sheet provided exactly what they needed: clear, efficient, and unambiguous MLA-style models for citing Internet sources.

Enter Edith Trost, from St. Martin's Press, who asked whether we would consider expanding our essay into a textbook. We would indeed—and now, after extensive research and online communication with our professional colleagues and New York editors, we're happy to offer you *Online! A Reference Guide to Using Internet Sources.*

We've tried to make *Online!* the latest word on working with Internet sources—but we know that it's the latest word as of November 1996. And we know as well that it won't be long before new kinds of Internet sources emerge, bringing new questions. Take those questions to our site on the World Wide Web at <http://www.smpcollege.com/online-guide>. There you'll find yourself among other writers and researchers who share an interest in writing well within webbed environments. We hope this site, and this book, will be practical and useful—helpful harbors for all who navigate the Internet.

To all who have helped us prepare *Online!* we give our thanks and appreciation. We especially want to acknowledge the help of Mick Doherty, the editor of *Kairos*, for encouraging us to publish the initial essay. We gratefully salute the staff of Eastern Kentucky University's Academic Computing and Telecommunications Services, especially Margaret Lane and Melvin Alcorn, for their abundant and generous assistance along the way. We say thanks to all the students in Honors Rhetoric who have asked great questions about the Internet. We acknowledge all who created and subscribe to the Alliance for Computers and Writing for sustaining one of the world's most informative and helpful listservs. To Michael Meeker of Winona State University and Stuart A. Selber of Texas Tech University, who reviewed portions of the manuscript and gave us valuable suggestions, we say, "Thanks upon thanks!" From the Bluegrass of Kentucky we bow eastward in deep gratitude to Marilyn Moller, Carla Samodulski, and especially Talvi Laev—our wonderful and able Park Avenue South editors whom we've come to know so well as friends and as the best of readers. Finally, we hug and cheer our families—our wives, Paula and Beth, and our children, Chelsea, Amy, Lisa, Kirk, Jonathan, and Benjamin, all of whom gave us the love, encouragement, and time to begin and complete *Online!* To all, a thousand thanks!

Andrew Harnack
<engharnack@acs.eku.edu>

Eugene Kleppinger
<actklepp@acs.eku.edu>

Glossary

This glossary appears at the beginning of *Online!* because understanding the language of the Internet is crucial to your use of this book. This language includes technical terms, jargon, and even slang, and some of it may be quite new to you. If you have little or no experience using the Internet for research, take some time to read through the glossary now. Later, as you come across terms or concepts that need clarification, you'll find help here.

You'll encounter many of these terms again and again as you use the Internet—and as you use *Online!* To make the book easy to use, all the terms in the glossary are highlighted when they're introduced in the text; whenever you come across a highlighted word, know that you'll find it explained in the glossary.

To learn more about topics covered in the glossary, visit the *Online!* homepage at <http://www.smpcollege.com/online-guide>.

< > (angle brackets) Angle brackets around text indicate that all the characters within the brackets must be treated as a single unit, with no spaces between parts, as in <http://www.infolink.org/glossary.htm>. By using angle brackets to frame handwritten or printed electronic information (e.g., email addresses and Web site locations), you prevent misinterpretation. Leave the angle brackets off such information when you type it into your browser's or email program's dialog box.

@ (the "at" sign) A fixture in every email address, @ separates the username from the domain name, indicating that you are "at" a particular electronic address.

1

For example, <jhsmith@acs.eku.edu> indicates that someone, possibly Jane Smith, gets email at Academic Computing Services, which is at Eastern Kentucky University, an educational institution. See also *email* and *email address*.

. (the dot)   The period symbol, called "the dot" in online lingo, is used to separate parts of email addresses, URLs, and newsgroup names, as in <jhsmith @acs.eku.edu>, <http://www.yahoo.com>, and <alt.sci.ecology>.

/ (the forward slash)   Used to separate parts of URLs, as in <ftp://ftp.tidbits.com/pub>; not to be confused with the backward slash \ used in DOS directory paths.

account name   See *username*.

Archie   An Internet search tool for finding and retrieving computer files from archives.

archive   A collection of computer files stored on a server. FTP sites are typical examples of archives.

article   Internet lingo for a message posted online.

ASCII   An acronym for American Standard Code for Information Interchange, ASCII is the most basic format for transfering files between different programs. It is sometimes referred to in wordprocessing programs as "unformatted text."

asynchronous communication   Electronic communication involving messages that are posted and received at different times. Email is an example of such delayed communication.

BBS (bulletin board service)   A service maintained by a computer that serves as an information hub for many computers. People with common interests subscribe to a BBS in order to post and receive messages.

bookmark   An entry in a bookmark list.

bookmark list   A browser's pull-down menu or pop-up window containing links to Web sites you want to visit frequently; sometimes called a *hotlist*.

browser   A World Wide Web program for navigating the Internet. Most browsers display graphics and formatted pages and let you click on hyperlinks to "jump" from one Web page to another. Widely used *graphic browsers* include HotJava, Microsoft Explorer, NCSA

Mosaic, and Netscape Navigator. A popular *text-only browser* is Lynx.

bulletin board service See *BBS*.

client A requester of information. As you surf the Internet, you, your computer, or your browser may be considered an Internet client.

cyber- A prefix describing something that has been created electronically and is available online (e.g., a *cyberworld,* a *cybercity,* a *cyberstore*). *Cyber* can also stand alone as an adjective, especially to avoid clunky compounds: *cyber rights, cyber cowboy, cyber pipe dreams.*

cyberography A list of references to Internet sites.

cyberspace The Internet; more loosely, the online world.

dialog box A window on your computer screen that prompts you to type something, make choices, or confirm a command before the program can continue.

digital Electronic; "wired."

direct access A computer connection that lets you use Internet software (e.g., a graphic browser) on your personal computer.

directory A list or collection of related computer files, sometimes called a *folder*. A directory may contain other directories, which are then called *subdirectories*.

directory path The sequence of directories and subdirectories you need to open to find a particular computer file. For example, the directory path <pub\data\history> shows that the *history* file is in the *data* subdirectory, which in turn is in the *pub* directory.

domain See *domain name*.

domain name The string of letters and symbols associated with a Web site or email service provider, as in <www.enigmacom.com>. A domain name has at least two *elements* (parts), separated by periods. The first element or elements uniquely identify an organization's server, while the final element, called the *domain,* identifies the type of organization operating the server. Common suffixes include *.com* (commercial), *.edu* (educational), *.gov* (government), *.mil* (military), *.net* (network management), and *.org* (noncommercial/nonprofit). Domains outside the United States often identify the country in which a server is located (e.g., *.au* for Australia, *.ch* for Switzerland).

download   To transfer information electronically from one computer to another, as when you move a program from an archive to your computer.

email (electronic mail)   Any of various programs that send and receive messages over a network.

email address   The address you use to send and receive email. Your email address contains your username, the @ symbol, and the domain name, as in <jhsmith@acs.eku.edu>.

emoticons   Small graphic renderings, composed of ASCII characters, that writers substitute for facial expressions and body language. Emoticons are useful in an online world where curt or hastily written messages can easily offend, and where you may want to indicate humor, surprise, or some other emotion to readers who cannot see you. Some of the most popular emoticons are :-) (smile), :-((frown), ;-/ (skeptical),} :-> (devilish), and :-o (surprised). For a fuller list, see *Emoticons* at <http://jwp.bc.ca/peregrine/irc/emot.htm>.

FAQ (frequently asked questions)   Pronounced "fack"; a file containing answers to common questions that new users of a program or service might ask. If you are new to a newsgroup or listserv, look up the group's FAQ file and read the answers to questions others have already asked.

FTP (file transfer protocol)   The set of commands used to transfer files between computers on the Internet.

GIF (graphics interchange format)   Pronounced "jiff" or "giff"; one of two common formats (the other is *JPEG*) for image files associated with Web documents. The acronym appears at the end of the filename, as in <marsface.gif>.

gopher   A program for accessing Internet information through hierarchical menus, gopher will "go for" the information you select and will display it on your screen. When you use gopher through direct access, with a graphic browser, you choose menu items by clicking your computer's mouse. When you use gopher through indirect access, the menu lists choices by line number, and you select what you want using keyboard commands. Gopher's text-oriented file format makes it especially useful for searching large collections of texts such as electronic books, library catalogs, historical documents, and specialized databases. On the World Wide Web, gopher addresses begin with *gopher://* instead of *http://*.

history list A list (usually a pull-down menu) of the Web pages you most recently visited. History lists let you return quickly to a site or see an overview of your latest surfing session.

hit In Internet lingo, hit can mean (1) an item in the list of search results a browser gives you ("Alta Vista's search for *scorpions* turned up sixty-nine hits"), or (2) accessing of a Web page by an Internet surfer ("The *Online!* Web page received three dozen hits this week").

homepage Usually the first page you see when you access a particular Web site, a homepage has hypertext links to other pages on the same server or to other Web servers. Both organizations and individuals can have their own homepages.

hotlink See *hyperlink*.

hotlist See *bookmark list*.

HTML (hypertext markup language) A computer code that allows you to create pages on the World Wide Web. HTML "tags" electronic text to indicate how it should be displayed onscreen by browsers. It provides a common language for browsers using different computer systems (Mac, PC, Unix, etc.).

HTTP (hypertext transfer protocol) The communication rules used by browsers and servers to move HTML documents across the Web.

hyperlink A connection between two places on the Web. Hyperlinks are represented onscreen by highlighted icons or text. Selecting a hyperlink makes your browser "jump" from one place to another. Hyperlinks are sometimes called *hotlinks*.

HyperNews A format that lets Web pages offer articles to read and gives readers special tools for responding online to articles and responses already posted by others. In HyperNews, all contributions are automatically added to the Web page, whose topically arranged menu gives convenient access to *threads* (ongoing discussions on specific topics).

hypertext A document coded in HTML; a collection of such documents.

hypertext link A connection between two documents or sections of a document on the Web; a type of *hyperlink*.

hypertext markup language See *HTML.*

hypertext transfer protocol See *HTTP.*

indirect access A computer connection that lets you run Internet programs stored on another computer system; also called *shell access.*

Internet A vast network of computers offering many types of services, including email and access to the World Wide Web. As a "network of networks," the Internet links computers around the world.

Internet service provider (ISP) A person or company providing access to the Internet.

IRC (Internet relay chat) The online equivalent of CB radio and telephone conferencing, IRC lets you communicate synchronously (in "real time") with other people. See also *synchronous communication.*

ISP See *Internet service provider.*

JPEG (Joint Photographic Experts Group) Pronounced "jay-peg"; one of two common formats (the other is GIF) for image files associated with Web documents. In filenames the acronym appears as *jpeg* or *jpg,* as in <pluto.jpg>.

keyword The term you type into a search tool's dialog box; what you want to search for.

linkage data Information about the hypertext context in which a document is located (i.e., the document's links to other documents).

listserv An ongoing email discussion about a technical or nontechnical issue. Participants subscribe via a central service, and listservs may have a moderator who manages information flow and content.

modem Equipment that connects a computer to a data transmission line (usually a telephone line), enabling the computer to communicate with other computers and the Internet.

MOO (multi-user domain, object-oriented) An electronic "space" in which many people can interact simultaneously. Accessible through telnet, MOOs enable classes, seminars, and friends to meet at a given time, usually to discuss a given topic.

MUD (multi-user domain) As electronic "spaces" for simultaneous communication, MUDs provide opportunities for role-playing in which each participant usually controls one character who has a complete life history and persona and can express a variety of physical and emotional responses.

netiquette A combination of the words *Net* and *etiquette*, *netiquette* refers to appropriate behavior on a network, and more generally the Internet.

newsgroup A group of people and their collection of postings on the Usenet network. Newsgroups are open forums in which anyone may participate. Each newsgroup has a topic, which can be as broad as the focus of <alt.activism> or as narrow as the computer applications discusssed in <comp.sys.mac.apps>. See also *Usenet*.

online On a network; on the Internet.

password A personal code you use to access your computer account and keep it private.

post To send a message to someone online. An online message is a *posting*.

protocol A set of commands—the "language"—that computers use to exchange information. Often-used protocols include FTP, gopher, HTTP, mailto, and telnet.

real-time communication See *synchronous communication*.

search engine See *search tool*.

search tool Any of various programs that work with your browser to find information on the Web. After you type a keyword or keywords into your browser's dialog box, a search tool looks for Web pages containing your keyword(s) and produces a menu of available documents (hits). Also called *search engine*.

server A computer that handles requests from client computers for data, email, file transfer, and other network services.

shell access See *indirect access*.

snail mail The U.S. Postal Service or another agency that delivers messages by courier.

subject directory   A hypertext list of available Web sites categorized by subject; what you get when you use search tools such as Yahoo! or The Internet Services List.

surf   To navigate the Internet. A *surfer* is an avid Internet user.

synchronous communication   Electronic communication in which people converse simultaneously with one another; also called *real-time communication.* MOOs, MUDs, and IRCs are examples of synchronous communication.

TCP/IP   An abbreviation for *transmission control protocol/Internet protocol,* TCP/IP controls software applications on the Internet.

telnet   A program that lets you log onto another computer from your own computer using a username and a password.

text index   A hypertext list of Web sites containing the keyword(s) you specify; what you get when you use search tools such as Lycos or Alta Vista.

thread   A series of postings about a particular topic. For example, you might decide to follow a *fire ants* thread in the newsgroup <alt.sci.ecology>.

URL (uniform resource locator)   Pronounced "u-r-l." A string of characters that uniquely identifies each page of information on the World Wide Web; a Web address. The URL for *Online!* is <http://www .smpcollege.com/online-4styles~help>.

Usenet   A network providing access to electronic discussion groups (newsgroups). You can join any of thousands of Usenet newsgroups by using a newsreader program.

Usenet newsgroup   See *newsgroup.*

username   The information that, combined with your password, lets you access your computer account; also called *account name, userid.* Your Internet email address probably begins with your username.

Veronica   An acronym for Very Easy Rodent-Oriented Net-Wide Index to Computerized Archives. Veronica is a program that searches for files over all available gopher servers on the Internet.

virtual   Online; occurring or existing in cyberspace.

WAIS (Wide Area Information Server)   A program that searches a variety of Internet databases by looking for specific keywords in documents rather than simply looking at document titles.

Web   See *World Wide Web.*

Web browser   See *browser.*

Web site   Any location on the World Wide Web.

webfolio   A collection of a student's texts published for review on the Web. Writing instructors teaching online often ask students to submit webfolios instead of printed portfolios. Businesses, craftspeople, and artists create webfolios to display their products, services, and artwork.

wired   Electronic; online.

World Wide Web (WWW)   A global Internet service connecting hypertext data and resources. Using a browser, you can move quickly from one Web site to another in search of information, graphics, and data.

To find out more about Internet terms, visit the *Online!* Web site or consult the following Web resources:

Wired Style
<http://www.hotwired.com/hardwired/wiredstyle>

Internet Glossary
<http://www.macintoshos.com/internet
.connectivity/internet.glossary.html>

Internet Glossary of Terms
<http://www.sparknet.net/spark_html/glossary
.html>

Web Info Internet Glossary
<http://www.infolink.org/glossary.htm>

CHAPTER ONE

Finding Internet Sources

You've probably seen the photograph from Mars showing hills that resemble a human face. Recorded by *Viking Orbiter 1* in 1976, this photo has been interpreted by some viewers as representing more than just hills and valleys— perhaps even representing the marks of an ancient civilization. Most scientists familiar with planetary photography dismiss such speculation; nevertheless, photographs of the "face" have become commonplace in the popular media, particularly the tabloid press, where scientific indifference to the potential significance of the "face" is sometimes interpreted as evidence of an official conspiracy to suppress "the real story."

If you wanted to investigate this controversy, you might begin with print sources—astronomy textbooks, NASA press releases, science magazines, and so on. You could interview a local astronomer or visit a planetarium. If you had access to CD-ROM photography archives (and if you had the necessary viewing equipment), you could see the Viking images for yourself.

Or you could turn to the Internet.

On the **Internet,** you could visit…

> The photo archive of the National Space Science Data Center at <http://nssdc.gsfc.nasa.gov/photo_gallery/photogallery-mars.html>
>
> The Alberta UFO Research Association at <http://ume.med.ucalgary.ca/~watanabe/guide/mars.html>
>
> Malin Space Science Systems at <http://barsoom.msss.com/newhome.html>

From these sites, you could print a copy of the official photograph (shown in Figure 1.1), read relevant press releases, find official NASA data, and create a list of references for future use.

A search of the Internet in July 1996 for sources related to the Mars face turned up more than 700 references, ranging from scientific photo archives to advertisements for T-shirts and watches bearing the Mars face. You could also consult with experts around the world by participating in **online** discussions about space exploration. In short, Internet sources offer a **virtual** grab bag of sources.

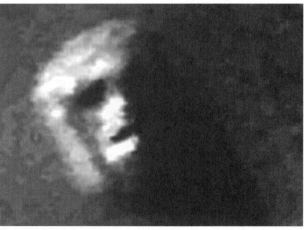

Figure 1.1
The "face" on Mars
<http://nssdc.gsfc.nasa.gov/photo_gallery/photogallery-mars.html>

This book will help you sort out the ones that will be useful for you.

Doing research on the Internet brings new opportunities—and new challenges. The Internet is *democratic:* all voices have an equal chance to be heard. The Internet is *global:* you can read an online document published anywhere in the world. The Internet is *up-to-the-minute:* facts and figures can be as fresh as the second you request them. The Internet is *interactive,* promoting communication as intimate as personal email and as public as online journals and Internet conferencing. Best of all, the Internet is *free:* the information found there costs absolutely nothing. (You may have to pay for access to the Internet, but the files you find are free.)

Because Internet publishing is at once democratic, inexpensive, global, and instantaneous (and because it often bypasses the formalities of print publishing), you need to be concerned about the reliability of what you discover there. Helping you evaluate the reliability of Internet sources is one of the goals of this book. (See Chapter 4.)

1a Understanding the Internet

The **Internet**—sometimes simply called the Net—links computers around the world. When you're connected to the Internet, you can communicate with people, schools, organizations, governments, businesses—anyone who has a computer with an Internet connection. In **cyberspace**—the electronic world you go to when you communicate with others by computer—you can listen to distant radio broadcasts, watch movie clips, play chess around the clock with someone in Russia, send email to a friend in South America, chat with colleagues every Tuesday evening, do research on any topic imaginable, contact manufacturers' hotlines—even shop for a used car.

So when you think of the Internet, think big. Imagine the Net as the communications mall of the world, a place where millions of people can communicate with one another. Like all large malls, the Internet has numerous entrances, information centers, levels, concourses, and specialized areas. Box 1.1 shows the cyberplaces—the virtual gatherings, events, information sites, and services—you can currently explore on the Internet.

Box 1.1
Visiting the Internet

World Wide Web Visit this service to find information and do research about people, places, events, and topics.

email (electronic mail) Use this option to send and receive messages on the Internet.

HyperNews Go to this service to read and respond to articles posted for specific audiences.

listservs Subscribe to this service to join ongoing discussions on specific topics.

newsgroups Go to this service to read and post messages to specific communities of people.

synchronous communications Go to these services to communicate with others live, in "real time."

telnet Use this service to log onto another computer from your own computer.

FTP (file transfer protocol) Use this service to transfer information from another computer to your own computer.

gopher Use this service's menus to find Internet sources.

1b Connecting to the Internet

Getting on the Internet is not difficult. All you need is a computer, a modem, and browsing software. A **modem** connects computers to phone lines; a **browser** helps you find places on the Internet. While individual computers may differ in how they are connected to the Internet, nearly all Internet connections provide the same basic services. Your **Internet service provider (ISP)**—perhaps your school's computer center, your telephone or cable company, a local or national commercial service, or a government or nonprofit organization—connects your computer to the Internet.

If you're connecting to the Internet from your home or apartment, enlist the services of an ISP. Your ISP will assign you a **username** (sometimes called an *account name* or a *userid*) and a **password**. Get the name and telephone number of a contact person to call at your ISP in case you have trouble connecting (e.g., if your password no longer works). Keep your ISP account information in a safe place. If you suspect your own computer is the source of your trouble, consult a computer technician.

If you're working with your own Internet connection, you can find help in Internet access guides, such as Adam Engst's *Internet Starter Kit* series for Macintosh and Windows computers. The *ISK* books are available in print from Hayden Books and are also published online at <http://www.mcp.com/hayden/iskm/book.html>, with related software at <ftp://ftp.tidbits.com/pub>. When you've made your Internet connection, go to Chapters 2 and 3 of *Online!* for tips about accessing specific Internet sources.

To learn more about the Internet, its history, how it works, or emerging Internet technologies, visit the following **Web sites**:

Walt Howe, "When Did the Internet Start? A Brief Capsule History"
<http://world.std.com/~walthowe/history.htm>

Internet Update
<http://www.itworks.be/ITUpdate/current.html>

Internet Update is a free online magazine, published every Friday, which looks at new developments, products, and trends in the cyberworld.

1c Navigating the Internet's World Wide Web

When you go to the **World Wide Web**, you enter a world of **hypertext** connections linking millions of electronic sites. Your computer communicates with such **Web sites** by following a set of basic rules called **TCP/IP (transmission control protocol/Internet protocol)** that provide a common language usable by all computer operating systems. **Browsers**—software programs that translate your keyboard-and-mouse activities into TCP/IP—find the multimedia information you seek and display it on your screen. When your computer retrieves information for you, it acts as a **client** working with **servers** (other computers).

The earliest Web browsers searched for and retrieved documents containing only text; today's browsers are also able to transmit images, sound, and video. If you connect to the Internet through **direct access** (described in Chapter 2), you can use a *graphic browser* that provides full-color images and easy-to-use menus for navigating the Web, saving and printing documents, and many other options. Popular graphic browsers include Netscape Navigator, NCSA Mosaic, and Microsoft Explorer. If you have **indirect access** (described in Chapter 3), you will probably use Lynx, the major surviving *text-only browser*.

Nearly all of the information available on the Web is published in **Web pages** composed of hypertext. Written in **HTML (hypertext markup language)**, Web pages contain **hypertext links**—usually represented by highlighted words or pictures—that alert you to the easy availability of more information. The links in a document may point to other portions of the same document, to other documents at the same location, or to any other document anywhere on the Internet. The hypertexts and their links form a three-dimensional electronic "web."

1d Understanding URLs

Every hypertext link contains a **URL (uniform resource locator)** that points to a specific Web site. Most URLs represent the address of a computer file or **directory** (collection of files).

1 Dissecting URLs

Here is how a typical URL looks:

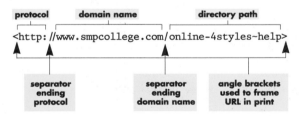

While some Internet humorists would have you believe that the abbreviation **HTTP** means "head to this point," it actually stands for **hypertext transfer protocol** . In a URL, the prefix *http:* represents the **protocol** (kind of link to be made). The two **forward slashes** after the colon show that the link will be to another computer. (URLs use forward slashes, never the backward slashes used in DOS directory paths.) The **domain name** identifies the owner of the Web site (in this case, St. Martin's Press); the last part of the domain name, *.com*, shows that the owner is a commercial entity. A slash separates the domain name from the **directory path**, which is the "address" of the part of the Web site that this particular URL leads to. **Angle brackets** separate the URL from surrounding text.

URLs for World Wide Web sites always begin with *http://*. Other frequently used Internet protocols and their prefixes include **FTP** (*ftp://*), **gopher** (*gopher://*), **telnet** (*telnet://*), **WAIS** (*wais://*), and the mail protocol *mailto:* (which does not use slashes). URLs for these protocols follow the *http://* pattern but often include other elements such as an **email address** or a **newsgroup** name.

To learn more about URLs, consult the Web document *Names and Addresses, URIs, URLs, URNs, URCs* at <http://www.w3.org/pub/WWW/Addressing/Addressing.html>.

2 Typing URLs

Take care when typing a URL because every letter, symbol, and punctuation mark is significant for computer communication; any extra or missing marks or spaces will prevent you from making a successful link. Always reproduce capitalization accurately. When showing URLs as part of text you're writing, enclose each URL in **angle brackets**—< >—for two reasons:

1. Enclosing a URL in angle brackets tells readers that everything within the brackets is part of the URL (even if the printed text breaks the URL in the middle so that it appears on two lines).
2. Bracketing a URL lets you use punctuation around the URL without introducing ambiguity about whether the punctuation is part of the URL.

The following sentence shows how angle brackets clarify where a URL begins and ends:

▶ For clear answers to questions about grammar, style, and usage, visit the Purdue On-Line Writing Laboratory at <http://owl.english .purdue.edu>; you'll especially enjoy its linked advice on punctuation at <http://owl.trc .purdue.edu/files/punctuation.html>.

URLs can be extremely long, running to hundreds of characters. In printed text, a long URL must often be divided. The following rules for breaking URLs are adapted from *Wired Style* (HardWired, 1996), written by the editors of *Wired* magazine:

- *Break a URL after the protocol abbreviation that begins it—http://, gopher://, ftp://;* don't break the abbreviation.

- *Break a URL before a punctuation mark,* moving the punctuation mark to the following line. (The following symbols function as punctuation marks in URLs: tilde ~, hyphen -, underscore _, period or dot ., forward slash /, backslash \, pipe |.)

- *As a last resort, break a URL in the middle of a word,* where you would normally hyphenate the word (but do not hyphenate the break).

Here are examples of acceptable breaks for URLs:

▶ `<gopher: //`
`gopher.inform.umd.edu/00/EdRes/ReadingRoom>`

▶ `<http: //lcs.www.media.mit.edu/people/asb`
`/moose-crossing>`

▶ `<http: //www.w3.org/pub/WWW/Address`
`ing/Addressing.html>`

Finally, when you enter a URL into your browser's **dialog box**, remember to type everything *except the angle brackets.*

1e   Narrowing a general topic

You can use the Internet to narrow a general topic to a more specific topic you want to research. Suppose you're interested in researching adoption. The Internet is rapidly becoming *the* major clearinghouse for adoption information because it connects people with sources on all aspects of adoption issues and permits quick exchange of information. **Surfing** Internet discussions of child adoption, you'll find a wide range of information, from scholarly expertise to personal pleas for help. One of the greatest achievements of the Internet is that it lets everyone's electronic voice be heard.

A preliminary Internet search on child adoption reveals many possible subtopics:

Searching for one's biological parents or children

Searching for prospective adoptive parents or children

Learning how to evaluate the health of available adoptees

Finding sources of support for adoptive families

Reading and analyzing stories about adoption

Working to improve adoption law

Each item on this list represents vast amounts of electronically published materials available in many forms. The main difficulty is not so much knowing where to begin—you could just go to the library and look up *adoption*—but knowing how to narrow your focus quickly, to browse through sources comprehensively yet efficiently. Although some very important resources such as legal databases and hospital birth records are not yet Internet-connected and must be accessed in more traditional ways, many adoption organizations provide Internet help in using such services. Internet tools for surveying and narrowing a topic are described in 1g-1.

1f Researching a specific topic

Sometimes you'll start your research with a fairly specific topic in mind. Suppose you want to know more about Charlotte Perkins Gilman's "The Yellow Wallpaper," a short story published in 1892 that recounts a woman's descent into depression and (perhaps) insanity as she struggles to express herself within her husband's agonizing restrictions. Because of its feminist elements and its powerful description of depression, the story appears regularly on reading lists for courses in literature, psychology, and women's studies. If you do an Internet text search for the **keywords** *yellow wallpaper*, you'll retrieve hundreds of **hits** (items matching your request), including many Web pages for classes where the story is being discussed. Among these pages is *The* Yellow Wallpaper *Site* at <http://www.en.utexas.edu/~daniel/amlit/wallpaper/wallpaper.html>, created to accompany an American literature course and maintained as an ongoing Web project. Through this page you can read an online edition of the story, find historical details about the author and the story's publication, read critics' comments and students' essays, select related Internet links, and even contribute to the ongoing discussion. If you leave a comment or ask a question, perhaps about the story's puzzling ending, your message automatically appears within the forum, and others can then reply to you the same way.

To see what other literary works are being explored similarly, visit the American Literature Survey Site at <http://www.en.utexas.edu/~daniel/amlit/amlit .htm> or search the Internet for the phrase *interactive texts*. For example, the Shakespeare Discussion Area at <http://the-tech.mit.edu/Shakespeare/cgi-bin/ commentary/get/main.html> houses evolving commentary on all of Shakespeare's works, with links to the complete texts.

1g-2 describes Internet tools for researching a specific topic.

1g Searching with Internet tools

You can use many different programs to search for information. Selecting the most efficient **search tool** for a particular topic usually means choosing between two kinds of tools: those providing **subject directories** and those listing **text indexes**. Subject directories are menus of topics and subtopics; text indexes let you scan documents for specific terms.

1 Tools for subject directories

Suppose you know the broad topic you want to research, but you haven't yet chosen a narrower subtopic to focus on. For example, you might be interested in child adoption but not know what subtopics were available for exploration. To find out, you could use one or more of the search tools listed in Box 1.2. All these tools index the

---

Box 1.2
Some popular subject-directory search tools

The Argus Clearinghouse <http://www.clearinghouse.net /searching/find.html>
Inter-Links <http://www.nova.edu/Inter-Links>
The Internet Public Library <http://www.ipl.org>
The Internet Services List <http://www.spectracom .com/islist>
Library of Congress World Wide Web Home Page <http://lcweb.loc.gov>
WWW Virtual Library <http://www.w3.org/pub/DataSources /bySubject/Overview.html>
Yahoo! <http://www.yahoo.com>

World Wide Web's contents by subject category and offer the results in a **subject directory** . This section describes some of the most useful subject-directory search tools.

Yahoo!
<http://www.yahoo.com>

Yahoo! is one of the most popular subject-directory search tools. Its **homepage** offers links to fourteen major categories such as Arts, Education, Entertainment, Health, Recreation and Sports, Reference, and Society and Culture. After opening a category, you keep choosing from successive menus until you reach a list of Web sites you may want to visit. Or, using the dialog box on the Yahoo! main screen, you can retrieve Yahoo! categories containing specific keywords, or individual sites whose titles or short descriptions contain your keywords. The list of **hits** for a Yahoo! search also offers links to other search tools.

If you asked Yahoo! for its subject listings under the category Adoption, you would get a list much like that in Box 1.3. If you clicked on Society and Culture:Families:Parenting:Adoption, you would get a menu that included Organizations. This hotlink would take you to a list of links to the resources of groups such as Adoptees in Search at <http://members.aol.com/denverais/adoption.htm>, the National Adoption Center (at <http://www.inet.net/adopt/nac/nac.html>, and the Surrogate Mothers Network (at <http://www.phoenix.net/~townhall/surrogat/surrogat.html>. The Yahoo! menu for adoption organizations probably doesn't include all Internet-connected adoption organizations because the database doesn't (yet) include every docu-

---

Box 1.3
Sample Yahoo! categories: Adoption

Business and Economy:Classifieds:Adoption
Business and Economy:Companies:Law:Adoption
Business and Economy:Products and Services:Children:Adoption
Business and Economy:Products and Services:Magazines:
Children:Adoption
Regional:Countries:Canada:Business and Economy:Companies:
Law:Adoption
Society and Culture:Families:Parenting:Adoption
Society and Culture:Lesbians, Gays and Bisexuals:Health:Adoption

ment available on the Internet, and because its index may place a particular agency's document in another category.

The Internet Services List
<http://www.spectracom.com/islist>

You might begin your Internet exploration with The Internet Services List, a popular subject-directory search tool. Its homepage has alphabetized links for approximately eighty topics, from Agriculture to the World Wide Web. Selecting a topic brings up a menu of further choices. Figures 1.2 and 1.3 show how the homepage and the list of links for Literature appeared in late 1996. Each underlined item on the list represents a link to more information, including other Web pages, gopher sites, and telnet connections. For example, selecting Project Gutenberg Master Index connects you to an online database of texts on a huge variety of subjects.

The Internet Services List does not pretend to cover the whole Web, but it offers excellent starting points for many subject areas, uses a relatively simple hierarchy, and leads to useful FTP, gopher, and telnet sources you might not find through search tools focusing on Web documents.

Inter-Links
<http://www.nova.edu/Inter-Links>

The Inter-Links homepage offers broad categories such as Topical Resources, News and Weather, and Reference Shelf. Clicking on these categories takes you to all the basic Internet search tools as well as onscreen help. The Web site's self-description "About Inter-Links" explains that "Care is taken to provide links to resources that are informative, stable (i.e., regularly accessible), primarily free and with a minimum of advertising, and likely to appeal to a wide range of people."

The Internet Public Library
<http://www.ipl.org>

The homepage of the Internet Public Library (IPL) recalls the lobby of a real library, with links to areas such as Reference, Teen, and Adult. According to the IPL's "Mission Statement," "The Internet is a mess. Since

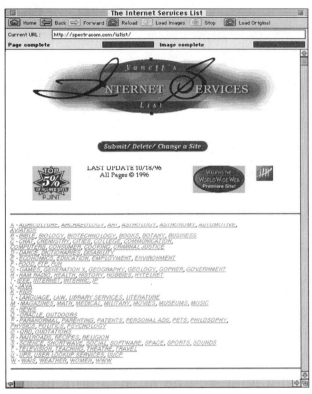

Figure 1.2
The homepage of The Internet Services List
<http://www.spectracom.com/islist>

nobody runs it, that's no surprise." The librarians propose to clean up the "mess," using their organizing skills to help people find and use information that is interesting and worthwhile. A special feature is the IPL Reference Center at <http://www.ipl.org/ref/index.text.html>. At this site, librarians will answer your questions by email.

Other subject-directory search tools At The Argus Clearinghouse, the WWW Virtual Library, and the Library of Congress World Wide Web Home Page, you'll find guides to Web resources for hundreds of subject areas. Typical subject guides include lists of Web, gopher,

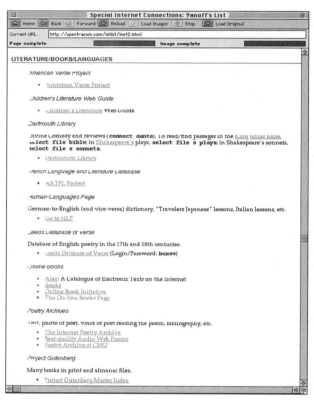

Figure 1.3
Links for the topic Literature from The Internet Services List

telnet, and FTP sites and listservs and newsgroups. The *Argus Clearinghouse* offers an especially wide menu of search tools at the Internet Searching Center at <http:// www.clearinghouse.net/searching/find.html>. The WWW Virtual Library, described by the magazine *Publishers Weekly* as "the granddaddy of sites on the Internet," has links arranged according to the topics used by the Library of Congress. You'll find the Library at <http://www.w3 .org/pub/DataSources/bySubject/Overview.html>. To examine one of the most extensive lists of Internet subject directories, visit the Library of Congress World Wide Web Home Page at <http://lcweb.loc.gov>, which has exceptionally useful links to search tools that provide information on all Internet sources.

2 Tools for text indexes

If you already know which aspect of a topic you want to investigate, you can use a search tool that scans the text of every document within its **text index** for the **keywords** you specify and prepares a results menu with links to documents containing the keywords. If you used a text-indexing tool to search for material about a broad topic, you might get an unmanageably long list of **hits**. For example, a search for the keyword *adoption* in 1996 with one text indexer produced more than 90,000 hits. Narrowing the search to *transracial adoption* reduced the number of indexed sites to fewer than 150.

This section describes some of the most useful text-indexing search tools; more tools are listed in Box 1.4. (For more advice on searching with such tools, see 4b-2 and 4b-3.)

AltaVista
<http://altavista.digital.com>

One of the most comprehensive Internet search tools, AltaVista indexes the full text of more than 30 million Web pages and several million newsgroup messages. You can perform a "Simple" search using the dialog box on the opening screen, or select an "Advanced" search screen that lets you specify more precise relationships among keywords and request that hits containing certain terms be listed first. You can also specify how much detail the list of hits should include. AltaVista generally gives more extensive results than other search tools, but you

---

Box 1.4
Some popular text-indexing search tools

All-in-One Search Page <http://www.albany.net/allinone>
AltaVista <http://altavista.digital.com>
Excite <http://excite.com>
Infoseek Guide <http://guide.infoseek.com>
Lycos <http://www.lycos.com>
Magellan <http://www.mckinley.com>
Net Search <http://home.netscape.com/home/internet-search/html>
Open Text <http://www.opentext.com>
Savvy Search <http://guaraldi.cs.colostate.edu:2000>
WebCrawler <http://webcrawler.com>

may have to look through many menus to find the most relevant items.

Open Text
<http://www.opentext.com>

Open Text gives you many ways to control the use of search terms—for example, by restricting the search for a particular term to a document's title or text. This method adds precision to the search, and the ranked results may provide more convenient access to important sources than AltaVista does, but the relatively small number of documents indexed by Open Text (about 2 million pages) means that you're likely to miss many relevant sources.

Lycos
<http://www.lycos.com>

Lycos indexes about 20 million Web documents. The main search page has a dialog box much like AltaVista's, while the custom search page lets you decide whether the match should be "loose," "fair," "good," "close," or "strong." These adjectives successively reduce the number of hits reported, but Lycos doesn't explain what the adjectives mean (e.g., how close a "close" match really is). You can also specify how many of your terms must be matched at once (e.g., "match 3 terms" or "match 4 terms") and how detailed the results must be. Documents are ranked according to how many of your search terms they contain.

Other text-index search tools   Netscape's Net Search, at <http://home.netscape.com/home/internet-search .html>, offers links to many other search tools. For novelty, you might consider the All-In-One Search Page at <http://www.albany.net/allinone>, which allows direct searching with more than 100 search tools, or Savvy Search at <http://guaraldi.cs.colostate.edu:2000>, which requests searches from several tools at the same time. Excite, Infoseek Guide, Magellan, and WebCrawler are other tools you may find helpful.

3 More about search tools

New Internet search tools appear almost every month, and existing search tools are continually being improved. As you encounter new or revised tools, be sure to check their Help documents for the latest developments and search hints. For up-to-date comparisons of search tools, consult the links within the Yahoo! menu "Comparing Search Engines" at <http://www .yahoo.com/Computers_and_Internet/Internet/World _Wide_Web/Searching_the_Web>. A thorough comparison of some common search strategies, "Great Web Searching: Tricks of the Trade" by Peggy Zorn, Mary Emanoil, Lucy Marshall, and Mary Panek, is available in print (*Online,* May/June 1996, 14–28) and at <http:// www.onlineinc.com/onlinemag/MayOL/zorn5.html>.

CHAPTER TWO

Connecting to the Internet by Direct Access

You can visit the **Internet** through **direct** or **indirect access**. You have **direct access** to the Internet if your personal computer (or the computer terminal you're using) has all the software you need to visit the Internet. You may have to connect to a network or dial into another system by a direct-access **protocol** (e.g., **TCP/IP**, PPP, SLIP or CSLIP), but after that you can use graphic **browsers** such as Netscape Navigator, Microsoft Explorer, Mosaic, and Eudora just as you use other programs on your computer. Web pages appearing on your screen will present both text and graphics. With additional software, you may also be able to hear sound effects.

Direct access lets you visit Web sources by following **hyperlinks** from **search tools** or from documents you've already visited. This chapter gives guidelines for accessing nine types of Internet sources.

2a Direct access to the World Wide Web

The **World Wide Web**—often called the Web—is a network of **hypertext** documents. (See 1c for a fuller description of the Web.) Each document has an "address" called a **URL (uniform resource locator)**. (See 1d.) Web page URLs always begin with the **HTTP** protocol, which appears in URLs as *http://*. For accessing URLs, most graphic browsers provide a selection in the File menu that gives you a **dialog box** with space for typing in a full HTTP address. To reach a Web site whose URL you know, type the URL into the box. (If you're working from within another text that contains the URL you want to reach, use your computer's Copy and Paste commands to insert the URL into the box.)

For example, to reach the **Web site** of Project Gutenberg, which is making classic texts available in electronic format, you would type:

▶ http://www.promo.net/pg

Figure 2.1 shows the Project Gutenberg **homepage**.

2b Direct access to email

Email (electronic mail) works like the postal system (only much faster!), transmitting messages to individuals and groups over computer networks. While you'll find many personal uses for email, in your research you will most likely use it for the following:

• Requesting information about authors and sources

• Using email links in Web documents

• Using **listservs**

Graphic browsers include all normal mail-handling functions. For example, with Netscape Navigator you can select the Netscape Mail window, then read or send messages. Mail-only programs such as Eudora offer specialized ways to organize your mail. A version of Eudora is available at no cost for Macintosh users at <ftp://ftp.qual comm.com/quest/mac/eudora> and for Windows users at <ftp://ftp.qualcomm.com/quest/windows /eudora>.

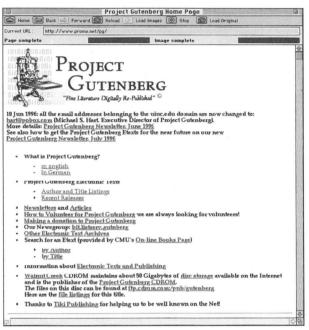

Figure 2.1
The Project Gutenberg homepage
<http://www.promo.net/pg>

2c   Direct access to HyperNews

HyperNews combines the hypertext of the Web with the discussion format of **newsgroups**. Each **article** in a HyperNews hierarchy has an ordinary-looking *http*: URL that lets you retrieve the article as you would any other Web page (i.e., by clicking on an onscreen link or typing into a dialog box). (To see how this works, look at Figures 2.2 and 2.3 or visit the HyperNews homepage at <http://union.ncsa.uiuc.edu/HyperNews/get/ hypernews.html>.) When integrated into a Web page's design, the HyperNews format preserves **threads** (series of articles about a particular topic) and lets you contribute responses that immediately appear as new articles under

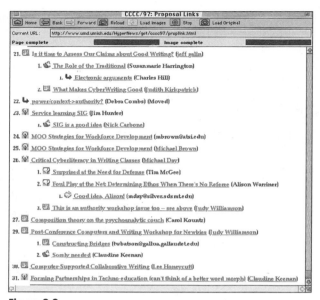

Figure 2.2
Part of the hierarchy of HyperNews responses for
<http://www.umd.umich.edu/HyperNews/get/cccc97
/proplink.html>

the relevant thread heading. In short, HyperNews gives you access both to an ongoing conversation and to the conversation's history.

If you use a graphic browser, you shouldn't need any additional software to access HyperNews materials.

2d Direct access to listservs

Listservs are ongoing email discussions about technical or nontechnical issues, covering the spectrum from aboriginal languages to zoology. Messages are typically announcements, questions, position statements, or replies and are distributed to the personal email boxes of all of the listserv's members.

In order to start receiving a particular listserv's **postings**, you must subscribe to the listserv from your own email account. *Important: Never send a listserv subscription request to the list's own address.* Listservs have a separate address for handling subscriptions, and sub-

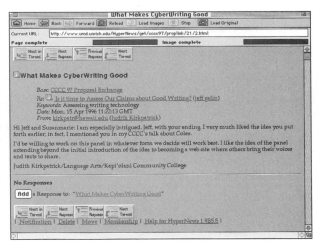

Figure 2.3
One of the HyperNews messages listed in Figure 2.2

scribers understandably become annoyed when they must sort out subscription requests from useful messages. As you uncover interesting listservs, pay careful attention to the *separate addresses for subscribing to a list and for sending messages to the list.*

For example, to subscribe to the Macintosh News and Information list, you would send the message *subscribe MAC-L* [your name] to <listserv@yalevm.cis.yale.edu>. To send messages to and from the list itself, you would use the address <mac-l@yalevm.cis.yale.edu>.

Listservs include *open lists* (to which anyone may subscribe and **post** messages), *moderated lists* (where a human moderator reviews messages before they go to subscribers), and *closed* lists (where you must request permission or explain your goals before being permitted to join). Discussions may range from technical analyses of narrow topics to friendly brainstorming. After subscribing to a listserv, observe the message traffic for a few days (or review the list's **archives**) to get a feel for the list's "personality" before contributing your own message. With most unmoderated lists, *anything* you send to the list address is forwarded immediately to every subscriber.

You can find information about listservs in most **subject directories** or in listserv indexes such as those listed on the Inter-Links "Email Discussion Groups" page at <http://www.nova.edu/Inter-Links/listserv.html>. If you're interested in a particular listserv, these tools can help you find the information you need to subscribe and to search the list's archives (if these are available).

2e   Direct access to newsgroups

The **Usenet** network provides access to many thousands of electronic discusssion groups called **newsgroups.** Unlike listserv messages (see 2d), which are delivered to your private email box, Usenet messages are collected on a system called a *news server*, where anyone with access to Usenet can retrieve them.

Here is a typical newsgroup name:

The first part of the name specifies the Usenet *hierarchy* (category) to which the group belongs—in this case, *comp.* for computer-related topics. A **dot** separates the hierarchy from the rest of the name, which specifies the news-group's topic through successively narrower subhierarchies—in this case, communications programs for Macintosh computer systems.

Other Usenet hierarchies include *rec.* for recreational activities and hobbies, *sci.* for scientific topics, *soc.* for social, political, and religious subjects, *talk.* for opinion, and *misc.* and *alt.* for topics that don't fit elsewhere.

Graphic browsers will accept URLs containing the news: **protocol**, as in <news:alt.adoption>, provided your menu's Options or Preferences specify a news server. (If you need to specify your news server, try the same address as your mail server or ask your system staff or **Internet service provider** for help.) Some browsers provide a separate window with Usenet-oriented functions. The browser retrieves and displays the messages you seek; it may also let you post your own messages.

If you can't use your browser to access newsgroups, you may be able to use a *newsreader* program;

try News Xpress for Windows at <ftp://ftp.tidbits
.com/pub/tiskwin/nx10b2.zip> or NewsWatcher for
Macintosh at <ftp://ftp.tidbits.com/pub/tidbits/tisk
/tcp/newswatcher-212.hqx>, or ask a computer expert
for help.

2f Direct access to synchronous communications

Synchronous communication allows two or more people
to participate in an ongoing online conversation, whether
they are socializing, playing games, or forming a "virtual
community" for learning. The simplest form of synchronous communication, a program called Talk, lets two people chat online, displaying their messages on the halves
of a divided screen. This "real-time" communication differs from **asynchronous** (delayed) **communication** such
as email because each person's message appears onscreen
as fast as it is being typed.

IRC (Internet relay chat), the online equivalent of CB
radio and telephone conferencing, is organized into chan-
nels where groups of people "gather" to chat. You can use
IRC by telnetting to a public-access client's address or by
finding a chat zone on the Web..

Among the most potent expressions of Internet inter-
activity are **MUDs** and **MOOs**, which provide electronic
"spaces" where people can "meet." **MUD** stands for
multi-user domain. If a MUD is *object-oriented* (meaning
that you can type commands to create and manipulate
virtual objects—tables, pets, or anything imaginable), it's
called a **MOO (multi-user domain, object-oriented)**.

The URL for a MUD or MOO site begins with theprotocol and usually ends with a port number.
Here's the URL for Diversity University MOO:

```
                protocol        site         port
                                            number
            <telnet://moo.du.org:8888>
```

Your browser can open such a URL as long as it can find
a telnet program (see 2g), but there are drawbacks to
telnetting to a MUD or MOO through your browser:
your screen shows all messages as a continuous flow,

and your own typing sometimes gets interrupted by others' messages, with very confusing results. If you must use this method, get advice from Nick Carbone's document "How to Survive with Telnet" at <http://www.daedalus.com/net/telnet.html>.

For frequent MUD or MOO exploration, you may want to use a program that gives you better control over what you type and what you see onscreen. Many programs are available for Macintosh, Unix, and Windows systems; for reviews, see Jennifer Smith's "Frequently Asked/Answered Questions" at <http://www.math.okstate.edu/~jds/mudfaqs.html>. Web pages that give information about basic MUD/MOO commands and describe various sites include Jeffrey Galin's "MOO Central" at <http://www.pitt.edu/~jrgst7/MOOcentral.html>, Andrew Sawyer's "Multi-User Domain Object Orientated (MOO)" at <http://dist_ed.alaska.edu/WWW/moo/moo.html>, and Lydia Leong's "The MUD Resource Collection: Index" at <http://www.cis.upenn.edu/~lwl/mudinfo.html>.

2g Direct access to telnet

Telnet is an Internet protocol that lets you log onto another computer from your computer. When you type a URL such as

```
<telnet://lib.med.cornell.edu>
```

into your browser's window, the browser looks for a telnet program on your system. You can help your browser find an appropriate program through the Options or Preferences menu. If you don't already have a telnet program, you can get one directly from the Internet via **FTP** (at no cost). A common Macintosh program, NCSA Telnet, is available at <ftp://ftp.tidbits.com/pub/tidbits/tisk/tcp/ncsa-telnet-27b4.hqx>, and a Windows program, EWAN, is available at <ftp://ftp.tidbits.com/pub/tiskwin/ewan102.zip>.

A telnet session opens in a new window on your screen. This window has no graphics and may show a blinking cursor awaiting your keyboard command. (Telnet can't send instructions from your computer's mouse to the computer you're trying to reach, although you may be able to use your mouse with your own software to highlight text on the screen in order to save it, print it, or copy it for use in your wordprocessor.) Once you're connected, watch for a message about an *escape character;* knowing the character will make it easy to end the connection when you're finished. As the session begins, you may get further instructions (e.g., "login as *visitor* and use password *guest*").

To end a telnet session, type the other computer system's escape command. If no command is listed, try *exit* or *quit* or press ^] or ^C (where ^ means that you hold down the Control key).

2h Direct access to FTP

FTP (file transfer protocol) transports files between computers on the Internet. Here's a typical FTP site URL:

You can type the URL command into your browser's dialog box. If you have only a site name, such as <ftp .tidbits.com>, construct a usable URL with the *ftp://* prefix: <ftp://ftp.tidbits.com>. If your browser responds "invalid URL" when you specify a site name, try adding a **forward slash** at the end of the URL: thus, <ftp:// wuarchive.wustl.edu> becomes <ftp://wuarchive.wustl .edu/>.

If you get a "login incorrect" message after attempting an FTP connection through your browser, the other computer did not accept your browser's automatic method for anonymous identification. (Most FTP **servers** expect your computer to use *anonymous* as your username and your email address as your password.) Consider using a separate FTP program (see the end of this section for advice), or try typing the expected identification as a URL in your browser's dialog box, according to the following special pattern:

▶ ftp: //anonymous:username%40system.dom@ftphost
  name.dom

The symbols %40 in the pattern represent the @ sign in your email address. (The @ sign itself has a different meaning when it appears in a URL.)

Although browsers are designed to handle FTP, you may have trouble in particular situations. One frequent problem with FTP arises when files in *binary* format are mistakenly transfered as *text* files, or vice versa. Binary files, such as programs or program archives, images, and formatted files from wordprocessors and spreadsheets, transfer more slowly than text files. Efficient file transfer depends on knowing the proper format for each file. The FTP process itself can't determine which kind of data a particular file contains; instead, it predicts which format to use from the *extension* (final element) in the file's name, such as *zip, txt,* or *html.* Currently, graphic browsers don't let you override these predictions, and so the transfer of a file with an inappropriate or unusual extension may fail or may make the file useless to you. If you have trouble using FTP through your usual browser, consider getting a separate program such as Fetch (for Macintosh) or WS_FTP (for Windows) for FTP. You can find Fetch at <ftp://ftp.tidbits.com/pub/tidbits/tisk/tcp/fetch -301.hqx> and WS_FTP at <ftp://ftp.tidbits.com/pub /tiskwin/ws_ftp.zip>.

For more information about using FTP, including detailed instructions for saving various kinds of files, see the document "World Wide Web: Telnet, Gopher and FTP" at <http://www.hsl.unc.edu/HSL/es/ntgftp.htm>.

2i   Direct access to gopher

Gopher, a program for accessing Internet information through menus arranged in hierarchies, will "go for" the information you seek and will display it on your screen. Gopher URLs look very much like HTTP and FTP addresses but usually contain a crucial one- or two-digit number that specifies the *type* of resource being selected, rather than just naming a file directory. For example, in the imaginary URL

▶ `<gopher: //domain.name.edu/7data/findit>`

the 7 signals a request to use the *findit* search within the *data* directory. Gopher selection pathways often involve characters, especially spaces, that are not allowed in standard URLs and so must be translated with special symbols, resulting in unwieldy strings like <gopher:// gopher.tc.umn.edu/11/Information%20About%20 Gopher>.

For URLs that begin with the *gopher:* protocol, use your regular Web browser. With a very complicated URL, you may find it useful to reach the "root" gopher by typing only the protocol and full server name (in this case, <gopher://gopher.tc.umn.edu>). When you reach the gopher site, use the menus to find the document by deciphering the correct screen selections from the remainder of the URL.

The fundamental search tool for gopher documents, **Veronica**, can be accessed through Web search programs such as Yahoo! and through the Veronica gateway at <http://www.scs.unr.edu/veronica.html>. Although some Web search results include gopher sources, the indexing of gopher sites is not complete, and you may find a separate Veronica search very helpful.

If you're not satisfied with your Web browser's handling of gopher sources, consider using a separate program such as WSGopher for Windows at <gopher://boombox.micro.umn.edu/59/gopher/Win dows/wsg-12> or TurboGopher for Macintosh at <ftp://boombox.micro.umn.edu/pub/gopher /Macintosh-TurboGopher>.

CHAPTER THREE

Connecting to the Internet by Indirect Access

You can visit the **Internet** through **indirect** or **direct access**. You have **indirect access** (sometimes called *shell access*) if you use a personal computer or networked terminal to log onto another computer (sometimes called a *local host*) and run programs on that computer. Indirect access usually involves typing commands at a prompt (such as a $ sign, a % sign, or a system name) or making selections from an onscreen menu. Your menu choices typically include Mail, Pine, Lynx, **FTP**, **gopher**, and **telnet** (and perhaps **WWW**, for **World Wide Web**). Your account entitles you to use a specific amount of disk space (often called your *quota*) for storing your own files at the other computer. The main limitation of indirect access is that it doesn't provide a *graphic interface,* which means that although you can access the text of Web documents, you can't see or use any graphics they may include.

Although indirect accounts don't connect you to the graphics and sound available on the Web, they do have some advantages. First, they're usually free (since they tend to be provided by colleges, universities, and libraries). Furthermore, while graphic **browsers** such as Microsoft Explorer and Netscape Navigator let you see the exciting visual displays that often accompany information, many researchers prefer to use text-only browsers such as Lynx, which retrieve information more quickly, bypassing the laborious **downloading** of graphics. (See Box 3.1 for a list of Lynx commands.) Even some researchers who do have direct access turn off their browser's ability to retrieve images so that they can gather Internet information more efficiently and print it (or copy it into other documents) more quickly. You'll discover that the Internet's treasury of information, opinion, and data is immensely valuable no matter how you access it.

Most software for indirect access is built to use *vt100 terminal emulation,* meaning that the software expects to receive commands typed at a terminal keyboard. Find the vt100 setting on your communication program's menu and use it. If you have trouble connecting, get help from your system staff or consider changing your communication software.

This chapter explains how to reach nine types of Internet sources through indirect access. (You may want to compare each section with the corresponding one in Chapter 2 to see how the addition of graphics changes the use of these sources.)

3a   Indirect access to the World Wide Web

The **World Wide Web**—often called the Web—is a network of **hypertext** documents. (See 1c for a fuller description of the Web.) Each document has an "address" called a **URL (uniform resource locator)**. (See 1d.) **Web page** URLs always begin with the **HTTP** protocol, which appears in URLs as *http://.* (Many Web sites are publicized without the protocol—for example, a television commercial might advertise <www.mci.com> instead of <http://www.mci.com>. When typing a URL, remember to add the *http://* prefix.)

Indirect access to the World Wide Web lets you retrieve all the *text* information at any given Web site. If you have indirect access, your browser is probably *Lynx*. To access Lynx, type *lynx* at your system prompt, or select Lynx from your menu. The first time you use Lynx, go to the Options screen (press o) to name your **bookmark list** and record your **email address**, and then save your changes (press >). The address for the first page you see when starting Lynx is usually set in the files that control your account; if you need to change it, get help from your system personnel.

When working with Lynx, you use keyboard commands, not mouse movements, to control its operations. For example, when you are using **hyperlinks**, which appear as highlighted text on your screen, you press the Down Arrow key to select the next available link and the Right Arrow key to retrieve the information from that link. Box 3.1 lists commonly used Lynx commands. (Your local system may use different or additional commands.)

Box 3.1
Basic Lynx commands

To see Help, press **h** or **?**.

To go to a specific URL, press **g**.

To add a bookmark, press **a** and then **d**.

To view and use your bookmarks, press **v**.

To delete a bookmark, highlight it and press **r** (on some systems).

To select a link, move the highlight bar with the up/down arrows or Tab, and then press Return or the right arrow. (If links are numbered on your screen as [1], [2], etc., you can select a link by typing its number.)

To see the next screen (which Lynx calls a *page*), press the space bar; to see the previous screen, press - (the hyphen).

To go to the end of a document, press **1** (the number one); to go to the beginning, press **7**. (These commands will not work this way if links are numbered on your screen, of course.)

To search within a document, press **/**.

To save, print, or email a document, press **p**.

To use a menu of pages you recently accessed, press the backspace key.

To see the Document Information page, press **=**.

To see the HTML source, press ****.

To quit, press **q**.

If the computer system you use for Internet access does-n't support Lynx, you may be able to use it through telnet (see 3g) by typing *telnet www.ukans.edu* at your system prompt and then following the screen directions. If you use telnet to run Lynx, you will not be able to save any bookmarks or changed options, and you will have to rely on the default bookmarks for searching and for entering URLs of your choice; the latter function is sometimes called *redirection* on bookmark menus.

3b   Indirect access to email

Email (electronic mail) works like the postal system (only much faster!), transmitting messages to individuals and groups over computer networks. While you'll find many personal uses for email, in your research you will most likely use it for the following:

• Requesting information about authors and sources

• Using email links in Web documents

• Using **listservs**

Although Lynx can usually handle mailto: links properly by interacting with your system's mail program, it cannot read or send mail on its own. Your email program is probably Mail, Pine, or Elm, and you start the program by typing its name at the system prompt or selecting it from a menu. Consult your system staff if you need help.

3c   Indirect access to HyperNews

HyperNews combines the hypertext of the Web with the discussion format of **newsgroups**. Each **article** in a HyperNews hierarchy has an ordinary-looking *http:* URL that lets you retrieve the article as you would any other Web page. (To see how the HyperNews format appears in **direct access**, look at Figures 2.2 and 2.3 on pages 32 and 33.) When integrated into a Web page's design, the HyperNews format preserves **threads** (series of articles about a particular topic) and lets you contribute respons-es that immediately appear as new articles under the rel-evant thread heading. In short, HyperNews gives you access both to an ongoing conversation and to the con-versation's history.

You can access HyperNews sites through Lynx. With indirect access, you'll be able to use all the tools for reading, responding, and getting help, but you won't be able to see some of the details of how the discussion is organized (e.g., icons highlighting messages). If you have trouble with a HyperNews page, send an email message to the page's owner, whose email address usually appears near the bottom of the page.

3d Indirect access to listservs

See the discussion of **listservs** in 2d. To access listservs through indirect access, you simply need to understand how your email program works.

3e Indirect access to newsgroups

See the discussion of **newsgroups** in 2e. To reach newsgroups through indirect access, you'll probably need a *newsreader* program. Common choices include TRN, NN, and News; ask your system staff for help if you need it.

3f Indirect access to synchronous communications

For a description of **synchronous communication**, see 2f. You can participate in synchronous communications through indirect access. See the information about indirect access to telnet (3g) and consider using a MUD/MOO program suited to your system, such as TinyFugue for Unix/Linux at <ftp://ftp.tcp.com/pub /mud/Clients/tinyfugue>.

3g Indirect access to telnet

Telnet is an Internet protocol that lets you log onto another computer from your computer. A telnet site's URL may look like this:

```
        protocol              site
     ┌──────────┐    ┌───────────────────┐
     <telnet://lib.med.cornell.edu>
```

To gain indirect access to telnet, you can either

- start Lynx and use the *g* keyboard command to type in a URL, or

- type *telnet* and the site name at your command prompt, and then press Return, like this:

▶ `telnet freenet.buffalo.edu`

Once you're connected, watch for a message about an *escape character;* knowing this character will make it easy to end the connection when you're finished. As the session begins, you may get further instructions (e.g., "login as *visitor* and use password *guest*").

A telnet address may include a *port number,* which makes special features available by changing some details of the connection. If you use the Lynx method, a port number appears as part of the URL, as in <telnet://moo.du.org:8888>. For the telnet command method, seek advice on which of the following three common numbers to use:

telnet moo.du.org 8888

telnet moo.du.org/port=8888

telnet moo.du.org:8888

Some telnet sites give instructions for telnetting to them. Figure 3.1 shows the telnet site of Diversity University, a nonprofit organization dedicated to promoting education with its **MOO**.

To end a telnet session, type the other computer system's escape command. If no command is listed, try *exit* or *quit* or press ^] or ^C (where ^ means that you hold down the Control key).

3h   Indirect access to FTP

FTP (file transfer protocol) transports files between computers on the Internet. Here's a typical FTP site's URL:

<ftp://wuarchive.wustl.edu>

How to Connect to Diversity University

1. telnet to moo.du.org 8888 (note that there is no period before the "8888"; the 8888 is the port and must be included).

If you access the Internet through a VAX/VMS, the port has a different format, making the command: telnet moo.du.org/port=8888.

2. After reading the introductory material, type connect guest.

3. Use the Diversity MOO Commands to look around, speak to people, and move through the environment. If there is difficulty, type help at any time.

Figure 3.1
Instructions for telnetting to the Diversity University MOO
<http://moo.du.org/dumoo/how2con.htm>

FTP via indirect access involves using one of the two following methods:

1 FTP via Lynx

Start Lynx and use the *g* keyboard command to type in a complete or partial URL (e.g., <ftp://wu archive.wustl.edu>). Continue through the file hierarchy using Lynx keyboard commands. Entries identified as "text/plain" can be opened and read like regular Web pages. When you see the entry for a file you want to retrieve, use the *d* keyboard command to start receiving the file. This process moves the file from the other computer to your storage area (quota) on your local host. To transfer the file to your personal computer, use the download features of your communication software.

2 FTP via the command line

Type *ftp* and the site name at your system prompt. You will probably have to identify yourself to the other computer before you can find the file you want. To do this, type *user anonymous* and press Return; when asked for your password, type your email address. Follow the directory path, using the *cd* command, as in *cd pub*, and view directories with the *dir* or *ls* command. When you see the entry for the file you want, use the *get* command with the file's *exact* name. To end the connection, type *quit* or *bye.*

For example, to retrieve the file <ftp://ftp.far_away.edu/pub/info/help.list> you would follow these steps:

At your system prompt, type *ftp ftp.far_away.edu.*

When connected, type *user anonymous.*

For your password, enter your email address.

Read any messages appearing on the screen. If all goes well, you will see the words "guest login ok," after which you may proceed.

At the prompt (which usually ends in >), type *cd pub* and you will see the message "CWD command successful."

At the prompt, type *ls* and make sure there is an entry for "info."

At the prompt, type *cd info* to see "CWD command successful."

At the prompt, type *ls* and make sure there is an entry for "help.list."

At the prompt, type *get help.list.*

You will be asked to name the "local file"; you can keep the current name by pressing Return, or supply a name you prefer.

When you see "transfer complete," type *bye* at the prompt.

Like the Lynx method, this process moves the file into your file space on your local host, and you have to use the download features of your communication software to transfer the file to your own computer.

For more information about using FTP, including detailed instructions for saving various kinds of files, see the document "World Wide Web: Telnet, Gopher and FTP" at <http://www.hsl.unc.edu/HSL/es/ntgftp.htm>.

3i   Indirect access to gopher

Gopher, a program for accessing Internet information through menus arranged in hierarchies, will "go for" the information you seek and will display it on your screen. Gopher URLs look very much like HTTP and FTP addresses but usually contain a crucial one- or two-digit number that specifies the *type* of resource being selected, rather than just naming a file directory. For example, in the imaginary URL

▶ <gopher: //domain.name.edu/7data/findit>

the 7 signals a request to use the *findit* search within the *data* directory. Gopher selection pathways often involve characters, especially spaces, that are not allowed in standard URLs and so must be translated with special symbols, resulting in unwieldy strings like <gopher://gopher.tc.umn.edu/11/Information%20 About%20Gopher>.

To go to gopher by indirect access, you can either

• start Lynx and use the *g* keyboard command to type in a complete or partial URL, such as <gopher:// inform.umd.edu>, or

• type *gopher* at your system prompt (or select it from your menu) and then use Gopher's keyboard commands and screen menus.

Box 3.2 lists commonly used gopher commands. (Your system may use different or additional commands.)

Box 3.2
Basic gopher commands

For a complete list, press **?**.

To see help, press **?**.

To go to a specific site, press **o**.

To enter a URL, press **w**.

To add a bookmark, press **a**.

To view and use your bookmarks, press **v**.

To select an item, move the highlight bar with the up/down arrows or Tab, and then press Return or the right arrow. (If items are numbered on your screen as [1], [2], etc., you can select an item by typing its number.)

To return to a previous menu, press **u** or the left arrow.

To see the next screen, press the space bar; to see the previous screen, press **b**.

To search within a document, press **/**.

To print a document, press **p** (available on some systems).

To email an item, press **m** (available on some systems).

To see the Document Information page, press **=**.

To quit, press **q**.

The fundamental search tool for gopher documents, **Veronica**, can be accessed at
<http://www.scs.unr.edu/veronica.html>.

CHAPTER FOUR

Choosing and Evaluating Internet Sources

While Internet sources can be informative and valuable, they should generally complement information from traditional print sources, not replace print sources entirely. Printed materials (e.g., books, encyclopedias, journals, newspaper articles, pamphlets, brochures, and government publications) are indispensable sources for research on most topics. Unless you are instructed otherwise, use both print and Internet sources in any writing project that requires research. This chapter looks at issues you are likely to encounter when doing research on the Internet.

4a Using Internet sources in your writing

Calling your readers' attention to Internet sources in your writing can give your work a special flair and distinction. However, if you use Internet sources, you must be careful to evaluate and cite them properly. When using and documenting Internet sources, follow three basic principles:

1. In your writing, make clear to readers which source you are referring to and how you understand its relevance to your topic.
2. Whatever citation style you use (MLA, APA, *Chicago,* or CBE), give your readers enough information to enable them to retrieve the source material if possible.
3. In your research notes or portfolio, store the data you collect about your Internet sources. Whether you store your notes and portfolio materials electronically, on paper, or both, you must preserve accurate data about your accessing of Internet sources.

As these three principles emphasize, you should pay careful attention to the details of reference citations. If you want readers to trust what you write, you must give them enough information to enable them to review your sources. Citing Internet sources is especially challenging because the Internet itself is constantly changing. New and different modes of access appear so frequently that pre-Internet documentation methods are often inadequate.

As information technology develops, new documentation conventions are needed. Chapters 5–8 of this book explain how to document online sources. At the *Online!* **World Wide Web** site at <http://www.smpcollege.com /online-4styles~help>, students, teachers, and scholars meet to discuss documentation styles and find solutions for the problems researchers encounter in **cyberspace**. For the latest information about citation, visit the site often. If you have a question about your research, difficulty documenting a source, or trouble locating information, **post** your concern at the Web site. There we'll do all we can to help you find answers and solutions.

4b   Identifying useful Internet sources

Finding sources of information on the Internet is relatively easy, but evaluating their quality requires great care. Searching the Internet with a tool such as Yahoo! or Alta Vista, you're likely to get a list of potential sources whose quality and relevance varies greatly. The fact that a source is listed in a **subject directory**, linked to another Web page, or mentioned in an advertisement does not guarantee that it is reliable.

Deciding which Internet sources are most valuable for your project requires patience and practice because there are few, if any, standards regarding what may be published on the Web. Some computer system administrators and government agencies may try to restrict access to material they deem offensive. But such regulations, even if they could be enforced, would have no impact on the *truth* or *clarity* of claims expressed on the Internet.

Consider this: not only is there no editorial board for most Internet publications, there also is no market force to drive incompetent or untrustworthy publications off the Web. The democracy of the Internet is apparent from a Search Results screen, where each **hit** appears as important as all the rest.

Confronted by such anarchy, but knowing that *some* Internet information is reputable, you as a careful researcher should evaluate Internet sources by asking questions like these:

• Which sources are worth inspecting?

• What information is available about a given document?

• How should I represent my evaluation in my writing?

1   Deciding which sources are worth inspecting

The menus you generate by searching with the Internet tools discussed in Chapter 1 often stretch to many screens and include hundreds or thousands of items. The relevance of some items on the list may be obscure because the terms you searched for are located somewhere in the document's text and are not yet visible on your screen. After you open a document you can, of course, use your **browser**'s Find or Search function to see where in the text your **keywords** actually appear. Only as you examine the document can you begin to evaluate its usefulness and integrity.

As you review a list of search results, remember to create **bookmarks** for useful-looking sites and documents. If you're using a graphic browser, add significant Web sources to your **bookmark list**, placing source titles in appropriate folders for future reference. If you're using

Lynx, change the current bookmark file whenever you want to through the Options screen (press *o*), which provides a convenient way to organize bookmarks. (See 4c-1 for more on bookmarks.)

2 Refining your search

To refine or limit your search, go to your **search tool's** Help command (accessible directly from most search tools' screens). Alta Vista's Help link, for example, suggests many ways to broaden and restrict searches. Suppose you want to explore Web sites offering information on transcultural adoption. A text search for such sites in October 1996 turned up nearly 2,000 documents containing the word *transcultural* and 217,500 documents containing the word *adoption*. When the search was narrowed to *transcultural adoption*, the query produced just eleven documents containing the phrase. When the search was further narrowed to look for the words *adoptive parents* within those eleven documents, the field shrank to two documents—a very manageable number of sources to examine closely! While each search tool has its own means for refining or restricting a search, you should always be able to find a Help or Tips screen that explains the options.

3 Using additional search terms and search tools

If your search results are either too numerous for convenient reviewing or too few for your needs, see whether a closely related term produces more useful results. Using a wild-card technique (e.g., searching for *immigra** rather than *immigration*) usually generates more hits, while narrowing your topic by adding more search terms usually draws the most relevant hits to the top of the stack. You can also try a different search tool—perhaps the All-In-One Search Page at <http://www.albany.net/allinone>, or Savvy Search at <http://guaraldi.cs.colostate.edu :2000>. (See 1g-2 for more on these tools.) Different search tools will give you different results, since each tool has its own strategy and its own database.

4c Gathering information about your Internet sources

Once you have assembled a list of useful sources, the next step is to gather the information you'll need to use the source. Capturing this information immediately is vital for finding it again and will make it easier to cite the source in your writing. Because Internet documents lack covers, dust jackets, and title pages, you'll have to inspect a source carefully for the information you need. Box 4.1 lists the types of information you should record.

1 Recording and bookmarking the information you collect

When working with print documents, you may be in the habit of recording essential bibliographic data either by hand or by photocopy. For Web, **gopher**, and **FTP** sources, much of the information you need is readily available while you are viewing a file, either on the screen or on the Document Information page provided by your browser. As you find useful sources on the Internet, develop the twin habits of (1) recording the Document Information page for future reference, and (2) making a browser bookmark so that you can easily return to the source.

Recording the Document Information page Depending on the programs you use, you may be able to store this data directly on your computer, or email it to yourself, or print it out. If your browser doesn't allow you to save the doc-

---

Box 4.1
Information to record about an Internet source

Author(s)

Title of document

Electronic address

Date of publication

Date of access

Part or section heading or number

Other important information (e.g., type of email message)

ument information to a file, open a wordprocessor window and use the copy-and-paste method to put the data into a file. Because a document's URL is crucial for your work, you must record it with absolute accuracy; therefore, any electronic means of storage or printing is preferable to handwriting. Be sure to record the date you access each URL.

Your browser may not provide a Document Information page for a particular source. For example, Netscape Navigator and Lynx don't display such information for **telnet** sessions. In such cases, you won't be able to save a bookmark in the usual way. You can, however, find the URL for a telnet link from the page on which you found the link. Do this by placing your cursor over the link (if you're using a graphic browser) or highlighting the link and opening the Document Information page (especially useful with Lynx). Some telnet applications allow you to "log" the session so that you can save some of the reference information.

Bookmarking the Web site   When you find a useful Web site, open your bookmark list and store the site's URL for easy retrieval. By adding bookmarks to the list, you can create a list of sources you consider important enough to reexamine. Each document's name appears on the bookmark list, so that when you return to the list, highlight the name of the file you want to review, and press Enter, the computer retrieves the file for you. Using your browser's other menus, you can examine your bookmarks to find information such as a bookmark's URL and the date you accessed the bookmark.

If you share a computer with other users, your ability to make bookmarks may be limited, or you may worry that others will erase your bookmarks. Many graphic browsers let you save bookmarks from your current Web search to a file and later import them to the browser again. If so, you can carry your bookmarks on a floppy disk for security. Another, less convenient method is to use the copy-and-paste method to transfer URLs between your browser's screen and a text file in your computer.

2   Locating the correct title for a document

The most appropriate title for an Internet document is not always the heading that first gets your attention on the screen. Most graphic browsers show the document's actual title at the top of the screen window. Lynx displays the title in the upper right corner of the text window. If the onscreen title is obviously incomplete, or if you have doubts about its accuracy, look for the complete version in the Document Information window (which you can access from the View menu in Netscape Navigator or by pressing = in Lynx). If the window title is uninformative or otherwise unsuitable, select the first main heading on the Web page.

Some documents are listed by search tools with the designation "no title" or with only a URL. If a document doesn't have a title, you will need to provide one so that you can find the document easily on your bookmark list and also cite it properly later. Avoid using "no title" and similar designations as titles of documents; instead, follow these rules of thumb:

- *If the untitled document contains text,* construct an appropriate title from the first major heading or the first text line. Enclose the title in square brackets to show that it is your editorial construction.

- *If the untitled document is a graphic,* construct a descriptive title such as "Photograph of Albert Einstein" and enclose it in square brackets.

- *If you reached the untitled document through a link,* you may be able to construct a title from the text surrounding the link. Record the title of the linking page for use with the citation format for **linkage data**.

- *If the untitled document is part of a larger hypertext work* (e.g., a chapter in a story), record the title of the complete work and then refer to the untitled source by its text division. Use this method when a source's URL contains a number sign (#), as in <http://www.spec tracom.com/islist/inet2.html#LITERATURE>, the Literature section of the Internet Services List.

3 Looking for the author(s) of a document

Authors of Internet documents don't always make their names readily visible. If the name of the person or organization responsible for an Internet source is not stated clearly at the beginning or end of the document, try the following approaches before labeling the source "anonymous":

- *Look for the author's email address.* If the address is not clearly visible, use your browser's Find or Search function to locate the @ symbol (which appears in every Internet email address).

- *Consult your browser's Document Information window.*

- *Open the document's Source Information window,* which you access from the View menu in Netscape Navigator or by pressing \ (the backslash key) in Lynx. Look for lines that specify the "owner" of the document, and record any names or email addresses you find.

- *If you locate an email address but no personal name,* try to find the real name by "fingering" the address. *Finger* is an Internet function that may be available from your system prompt (if you have **indirect access** to the Internet), from software on your own computer, or through a Web site such as <http//www.cs .indiana.edu/finger>. Finger and similar tools let you match names with email addresses. For more information about using finger, see Andrew Starr's Web page at <http://www.amherst.edu/~atstarr/computers /finger.html>. While the information from finger and other such tools is generally reliable, remember that some Internet-connected systems don't respond to finger requests and some systems use email addresses that won't work with these search tools.

4 Finding a document's URL

Every Internet document has a unique "address," or **URL (uniform resource locator)**, which specifies how the document can be retrieved. Graphic browsers usually display the current URL in a window. Some printer settings let you record the URL on each printed page of text. If you use Lynx, you can choose an "expert" option that turns off the ordinary menu of commands at the bottom of the screen and lists the URL instead; then, when you print the text of the Lynx screen, the URL appears on the printout. But the easiest ways to find and record a document's URL are to use your browser's bookmark and Document Information window features (described in 4b-1 and 4c-1). Use the URL reported in the Document Information window unless you decide to shorten it (see the following section, "Shortening URLS").

Shortening URLs   In a URL, any material following #
(the number sign) represents a section or division of a single file. If you're producing printed text and want to min-
imize the number of long URLs you show in the text, you
can shorten a URL by ending it at the # sign and using the
section label as a text division (as you would the page
number of a printed book). For example, the URL

▶ <http://www.spectracom.com/islist/inet2.html#
  LITERATURE>

can be simplified to

▶ <http://www.spectracom.com/islist/inet2.html>

if you tell your readers that you're referring to the
LITERATURE section of this document.

Very complicated or long URLs can be shortened (and
the retrieval process simplified for your readers) if you
can supply enough information about the source through
linkage data notes. For example, the complete URL for
"Pentium Jokes at" <gopher://Alpha.CC.UToledo.edu
:70/00GOPHER_ROOT%3a%5b000000.ENTERTAIN
MENT.JOKES-STORIES-AND-MORE.COMPUTER
-RELATED-MATERIAL%5dPENTIUM.JOKES> can be
shortened to <gopher://Alpha.CC.UToledo.edu> if you
specify that the joke list is "Lkd. 'Gopher Menu,' at
'Internet Activities,' 'Entertainment,' 'Jokes' and
'Computer Related Material." Identifying and specifying
alternate paths is not always simple, particularly for
gopher items, but it can make your (printed) text more
readable.

Typing URLs   For rules about typing URLs, see 1d-2.

5 Keeping track of publication and access dates

Keep track of two dates associated with your Internet
sources:

- Publication date (sometimes listed as *revision* or *modification* date)
- Access date

An Internet document's *date of publication* is essential
for identifying the document, since a file with a given title

can be changed or replaced without a trace. Many Internet authors include a publication date (or a date of *last revision* or *modification*) prominently at the top or bottom of a page.

The *date of access* tells readers when you accessed the document. This date, which usually differs from the publication date, becomes very important when you want to quote from the source or use its data. When you state your access date, you are claiming that the document as reported was available at that particular time. But a document may later be revised or cease to be available. Consider this scenario: you cite a source with a "last revision" date of December 31, 1996. If the author revises the file and simultaneously updates the revision date, others using your citation to locate the file will find a different date and will thus know they're looking at a changed file.

Your browser may provide convenient methods for recording access dates. For example, Netscape Navigator automatically stores the creation and access dates for each bookmark. You can find these dates by opening the Bookmarks file from the Window menu, highlighting a bookmark, and then opening the Item—Properties window.

Occasionally—for example, when looking at a directory obtained through FTP—you will come across a document's *file date.* The file date represents the date the document was stored on a particular computer. It is *not* the same as the date of publication.

Some **search tools**—notably AltaVista—associate a date with each item found during a search. These dates show how recently the site was indexed by the search tool; again, they do *not* reflect the item's publication date. Always look for the publication date of an Internet source inside the document or on the Document Information page.

Be sure to record a document's publication and access dates as accurately as possible.

6 Understanding site ratings

Various organizations such as Excite at <http://excite .com>, Magellan at <http://www.mckinley.com>, and the Argus Clearinghouse at <http://www.clearinghouse.net> offer ratings of Web sites. These ratings are often featured on the rated pages themselves. Don't let a rating claim interfere (positively or negatively) with your judgment of a site's reliability. Ratings often focus primarily on the presentation and organization of the information rather than on its reliability. For example, Magellan awards up to four "stars" to Web sites that qualify according to the following standards (listed under "How are the sites rated?" in Magellan's FAQ at <http://www.mckinley .com/feature.cgi?faq_bd>:

> *Depth:* Is [the site] comprehensive and up-to-date?

> *Ease of exploration:* Is it well-organized and easy to navigate?

> *Net appeal:* Is it innovative? Does it appeal to the eye or the ear? Is it funny? Is it hot, hip, or cool? Is it thought-provoking? Does it offer a new technology or a new way of using technology?

An award that emphasizes how "funny" a site might be should not be taken as evidence that the source's content has been evaluated thoroughly.

4d Evaluating the reliability of an Internet source

The Web contains a growing number of documents to help you evaluate the sources you encounter. An example is the subject guide "Evaluation of Information Sources" by Alastair Smith at <http://www.vuw.ac.nz/~agsmith /evaln/evaln.htm>. One of the best summaries of the evaluation process is Elizabeth Kirk's document "Evaluating Information Found on the Internet" at <http://milton.mse.jhu.edu:8001/research/education/net .html>. Kirk identifies five major criteria for evaluating all forms of information:

1 Authorship

To find out more about the *authorship* of an Internet document, consider searching for the author's name on the Web or in Usenet. (With Alta Vista, for example, you simply type in the author's name and request a Web or Usenet search for text containing information. If the

author maintains a homepage, it will be listed.) If bio-
graphical links are available, follow them; if the author
encourages contact via email, consider the offer seriously.
Most Web authors appreciate hearing from people who
make use of their information, and the Internet provides
a mechanism for responding that most print publications
cannot match. An author's homepage may contain helpful information, but comments from others about the
author's work are useful as well. Your goal is to establish
the author's qualifications for making the claims you
want to use.

2 Publishing body

The *publishing body* for an Internet document is the **server**
on which the file is stored, but there is no way for the
server to guarantee the reliability of the information it
stores. More important than the server's name are any
names or logos appearing within the document that represent organizations that may stand behind the author's
work. For example, you can be confident that Leslie
Harris's essay "Writing Spaces: Using MOOs to Teach
Composition and Literature," which appeared in *Kairos:
A Journal for Teaching Writing in Webbed Environments*
(Summer 1996), is valuable. *Kairos,* an electronic journal
sponsored by the Alliance for Computers and Writing,
has an international reputation for publishing articles of
high quality.

3 Referral to and/or knowledge of other sources

Understanding the author's *"referral to and/or knowledge of
other sources"* is probably the key to estimating the reliability of Internet source material. To find evidence that
will help you make this judgment, you can use two
approaches:

1. Examine the content of the document to see whether it
   represents other sources fairly.
2. Seek out other sources to see if the author has considered enough alternative views.

Of course, you may need guidance from others in the
author's field in order to make an informed judgment.
Here the Internet can play a key role by enabling you to
search quickly for the names or ideas of others mentioned
by the author. For example, you might subscribe to a **list-**

serv or participate in a **newsgroup** in the author's field, both to learn more about the context of the author's work and to be able to seek others' opinions if necessary.

4 Accuracy or verifiability

How you establish the *accuracy* of data you find on the Internet is not very different from how you establish the accuracy of print data, but the special features of **hypertext** often make your task easier. For example, an author quoting statistics from another Internet source will often include a direct link to the other source. Even though Internet sources that point to other documents in this fashion may not have traditional bibliographies, they are nonetheless well documented.

5 Currency

The *currency* of an Internet document refers to the history of its publication and any revisions. A document with no dating at all is less reliable (on this particular score) than one that lists numerous revisions; in the second case, the author shows greater respect for readers' information needs.

4e Representing your evaluation in your writing

When you use an Internet source in your writing, demonstrate your evaluation of the source's reliability by carefully choosing a *signal verb* to show your understanding of the author's purpose (what the author is trying to achieve in his or her writing) and how successful the author is in achieving that purpose. By using signal verbs, you let readers know the context in which the source's statement should be viewed.

Consider the following quotation from a message that Jeremy Abrams posted in 1996 to the newsgroup <alt.philosophy.objectivism>:

> Science offers no substitute for the ethical concern of religion.

You can introduce your use of this quotation with a variety of signal verbs:

Jeremy Abrams *says* that...

Jeremy Abrams *believes* that...

Jeremy Abrams *claims* that...

Jeremy Abrams *argues* that...

Jeremy Abrams *proves* that...

Your choice of the signal verb helps your reader understand both Abrams's intention and the degree to which he affirms and supports his statements. If you choose to use *proves* instead of *believes,* then you signal to your reader that the quotation in context proves by convincing evidence and persuasive logic that "science offers no substitute for the ethical concern of religion." If you choose the signal verb *say* instead of *prove,* you are reporting that Abrams makes his statement without any substantial support. Choose your signal verbs carefully so that they genuinely reflect the tone and substance of each cited source.

Box 4.2 lists some signal verbs you can use to show your readers how you have evaluated your sources. By using signal verbs to introduce and discuss Internet and print sources, you add integrity to your authorial voice and encourage your readers to trust the judgments you make in reporting and evaluating information.

Box 4.2
Signal verbs for evaluating sources

acknowledges	discusses	recognizes
advises	embraces	regards
agrees	emphasizes	remarks
allows	explains	replies
analyzes	expresses	reports
answers	holds	responds
appreciates	implies	reveals
asserts	interprets	says
assumes	leaves us with	states
believes	lists	suggests
charges	objects	supports
claims	observes	tells us
considers	offers	thinks
criticizes	opposes	wants to
declares	points to	wishes
describes	presents	wonders
disagrees	proposes	

Using MLA Style to Cite and Document Sources

This chapter's guidelines for citing Internet sources are based on the principles presented in the fourth edition of the *MLA Handbook for Writers of Research Papers,* by Joseph Gibaldi. MLA style advises that you acknowledge sources "by keying brief parenthetical citations in your text to an alphabetical list of works that appears at the end of the paper" (xiii). Widely used by writers in literature, language studies, and other fields in the humanities, the MLA style of documentation allows writers to keep texts "as readable and as free of disruptions as possible" (105).

The *MLA Handbook* provides information about the purposes of research; suggestions for choosing topics; recommendations for using libraries; guidance for composing outlines, drafts, notes, and bibliographies; and advice on spelling, punctuation, abbreviations, and other stylistic matters. It also presents a style for documenting sources and gives directions for citing print sources in the text and preparing a list of Works Cited. Thorough acquaintance with the *MLA Handbook* will, as its author promises, "help you become a writer whose work deserves serious consideration" (xiii). This chapter follows the conventions of MLA citation style.

5a   Adapting MLA style to cite Internet sources

Although the *MLA Handbook* provides tentative guidelines for citing "other sources" such as postings on electronic networks, its 1995 publication date precludes discussion of most Internet sources. The following recommendations adapt the *MLA Handbook*'s guidelines and models to Internet sources.

1   Link an in-text citation of an Internet source to a corresponding entry in the Works Cited.

According to the *MLA Handbook,* each text reference to an outside source must point clearly to a specific entry in the list of Works Cited. The essential elements of an in-text citation are the author's name (or the document's title, if no author is identified) and a page reference or other information showing where in a source cited material appears.

Create an in-text reference to an Internet source by using a signal phrase, a parenthetical citation, or both a previewing sentence and a parenthetical citation.

Using a signal phrase   To introduce cited material consisting of a short quotation, paraphrase, or summary, use either a signal phrase set off by a comma or a signal verb with a *that* clause, as in the following examples. (See 4e for a discussion of signal phrases and verbs.)

Box 5.1
Using italics and underlining in MLA style

MLA style recommends italicizing certain elements (e.g., book and journal titles) in printed text and underlining them in manuscript. The use of underlining to represent italics becomes a problem when you compose texts for online publication. On the World Wide Web, underlining in a document indicates that the underlined word or phrase is an active hypertext link. (All HTML editing programs automatically underline any text linked to another hypertext or Web site.)

When composing Web documents, avoid underlining. Instead, use italics for titles, for emphasis, and for words, letters, and numbers referred to as such. When you write with programs such as email that don't allow italics, type an underscore mark _like this_ before and after text you would otherwise italicize or underline.

signal phrase

▶ According to Daniel LaLiberte, HyperNews is "a cross between the hypermedia of the WWW and Usenet News."

signal phrase

▶ In his January 1991 letter to the editors of PMLA, Jason Mitchell suggests that the "pretentious gibberish" of modern literary critics-- "Eurojive," as he calls it--is often produced by English professors who need to prove that their professional status is equal to that of math and science faculty.

Here are the Works Cited entries for these two sources:

▶ LaLiberte, Daniel. <liberte@ncsa.uiuc.edu>
    "What Is HyperNews?" 16 Feb. 1996. Base
    article. <http://union.ncsa.uiuc.edu
    /HyperNews/get/hypernews/about.html>
    (14 May 1996).

▶ Mitchell, Jason P. "PMLA Letter." 1991. <http://
    sunset.backbone.olemiss.edu/~jmitchel/pmla
    .htm> (23 May 1996).

Using a parenthetical citation To identify the source of a quotation, paraphrase, or summary, place the author's last name in parentheses after the cited material.

▶ "Welcome to HyperNews" [with] its associated links is a helpful introduction because it provides a history of the program's evolution, installation instructions, and commentary about its future use (LaLiberte).

▶ In response to Victor Brombert's 1990 MLA presidential address on the "politics of critical language," one correspondent suggests that "some literary scholars envy the scientists their wonderful jargon with its certainty and precision and thus wish to emulate it by creating formidably technical-sounding words of their own" (Mitchell).

Here are the Works Cited entries for these sources:

▶ LaLiberte, Daniel. <liberte@ncsa.uiuc.edu> "What
    Is HyperNews?" 16 Feb. 1996. Base article.
    <http://union.ncsa.uiuc.edu/HyperNews/get
    /hypernews/about.html> (14 May 1996).

▶ Mitchell, Jason P. "PMLA Letter." 1991. <http://
    sunset.backbone.olemiss.edu/~jmitchmla.htm>
    (23 May 1996).

Using a previewing sentence and a parenthetical citation
To introduce and identify the source of a long quotation
(one comprising more than four lines in your essay or
research paper), use a previewing sentence that ends in a
colon. By briefly announcing the content of an extended
quotation, a previewing sentence tells readers what to
look for in the quotation. Indent the block quotation ten
spaces (or two paragraph indents) from the left margin.
At the end of the block quotation, cite the source in parentheses after the final punctuation mark.

▶ That the heroic and historically important deeds of previ-
    ously unknown women should be included in history
    books is evident from the following notice:

> Event: April 26, 1777, Sybil Ludington. On
> the night of April 26, 1777, Sybil
> Ludington, age 16, rode through towns in
> New York and Connecticut to warn that the
> Redcoats were coming . . . to Danbury,
> CN. All very Paul Reverish, except Sybil
> completed HER ride, and SHE thus gathered
> enough volunteers to help beat back the
> British the next day. Her ride was twice
> the distance of Revere's. No poet immor-
> talized (and faked) her accomplishments,
> but at least her hometown was renamed
> after her. However, recently the National
> Rifle Association established a Sybil
> Ludington women's "freedom" award for mer-
> itorious service in furthering the purpos-
> es of the NRA as well as use of firearms
> in competition or in actual life threaten-
> ing situations although Sybil never fired
> a gun. (Stuber)

Here is the Works Cited entry:

▶ Stuber, Irene. "April 23, 1996: Episode 635."
     <u>Women of Achievement and Herstory: A</u>
     <u>Frequently-Appearing Newsletter.</u> 3 May
     1996. <http://worcester.lm.com/women/is
     /achievement.html> (30 May 1996).

2 Substitute Internet text divisions for page numbers.

The examples in 5a-1 assume that an Internet source has
no internal divisions (pages, parts, chapters, headings,
sections, subsections). The *MLA Handbook*, however,
requires that you identify the location of any cited information as precisely as possible in parentheses. Because
Internet sources are rarely marked with page numbers,
you will not always be able to show exactly where cited
material comes from. If a source has internal divisions,
use these instead of page numbers in your citation. Be
sure to use divisions inherent in the document and not
those provided by your browsing software.

A text reference to a source with divisions may
appear in the text along with the author's name or be
placed in parentheses after a quotation, paraphrase, or
summary.

▶ As TyAnna Herrington notes in her Introduction,
   "Nicholas Negroponte's <u>Being Digital</u> provides
   another welcome not only into an age of technological ubiquity, but into a way of 'being'
   with technology."

▶ "Negroponte's uncomplicated, personal tone fools
   the reader into a sense that his theses are
   simplistic" (Herrington "Introduction").

Here is the Works Cited entry:

▶ Herrington, TyAnna K. "Being Is Believing."
     Rev. of <u>Being Digital</u>, by Nicholas
     Negroponte. <u>Kairos: A Journal for Teaching</u>
     <u>Writing in Webbed Environments</u> 1.1 (1996)
     <http://129.118.38.138/kairos/1.1> (24 May
     1996).

3   Use source-reflective statements to show where cited material ends.

The MLA practice of parenthetical page-number citation lets you indicate precisely where information from a printed source ends. Many Internet sources, however, appear as single screens, and MLA style does not require parenthetical page citations for one-page works. By analogy, a single-screen document cited in text needs no page citation. To let your readers know where your use of an Internet source with no text divisions ends, use a source-reflective statement.

Source-reflective statements give you an opportunity to assert your authorial voice. Writers use source-reflective statements to provide editorial comment, clarification, qualification, amplification, dissent, agreement, and so on. In the following example, the absence of a source-reflective statement creates uncertainty as to where use of an Internet source ends.

▶ According to TyAnna Herrington, Nicholas
  Negroponte has the ability to make complex
  technological issues understandably simple. For
  those who are not techno-philes, this is a
  blessing; it allows them to apprehend the real
  significance of digital technology without feeling that such ideas are too difficult to consider.

In the next example, the writer has added a source-reflective statement to show that use of the source has ended.

source-reflective statement

▶ According to TyAnna Herrington, Nicholas
  Negroponte has the ability to make complex
  technological issues understandably simple.
  Herrington's observation is a good one.
  It means that for those who are not techno-
  philes, reading Negroponte is a blessing; reading Negroponte allows one to apprehend the real
  significance of digital technology without
  feeling that such ideas are too difficult to
  consider.

Here is the Works Cited entry:

▶ Herrington, TyAnna K. "Being Is Believing."
         Rev. of <u>Being Digital</u>, by Nicholas
         Negroponte. <u>Kairos: A Journal for Teaching</u>
         <u>Writing in Webbed Environments</u> 1.1 (1996)
         <http://129.118.38.138/kairos/1.1> (24 May
         1996).

5b Works Cited

When using MLA style, place a list of cited sources, arranged alphabetically, after the text of your essay and any explanatory notes. The *MLA Handbook* recommends that you "draft the [Works Cited] section in advance, so that you will know what information to give in parenthetical references as you write" (106). Doing this makes in-text citation of sources easier by giving you an idea of what in-text reference options will work best for each citation.

Referring to print sources, the *MLA Handbook* gives the following general models for Works Cited entries:

Book

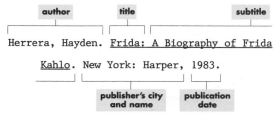

Periodical article

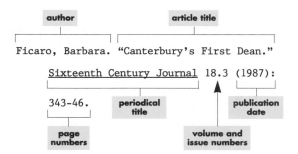

Box 5.2
Using hypertext to document sources on the Web

The hypertext environment of the World Wide Web doesn't just alter the way you do research, it also lets you document sources in a new way—by using hypertext links. Electronic journals published on the Web are already replacing traditional notes, Works Cited listings, appendixes, and other supporting text with links to the documents being cited. To read more about hypertext documentation, see 10f in this book. For an example of how it works, look at the format of Andrew Harnack and Eugene Kleppinger, "Beyond the *MLA Handbook*: Documenting Electronic Sources on the Internet" in *Kairos: A Journal for Teaching Writing in Webbed Environments* 1.2 (1996) at <http://english.ttu.edu/kairos/1.2 /inbox/mla.html> or any essay published in *Kairos* at <http:// english.ttu.edu/kairos>.

The *MLA Handbook* also presents numerous variations that accommodate a variety of print sources (e.g., a multivolume work, an editorial). For detailed information on creating a Works Cited list, see Chapter 4 of the *MLA Handbook,* "Documentation: Preparing the List of Works Cited."

Extending the citation practice of the *MLA Handbook* to include Internet sources produces the following model:

Online document

▶ Author's name (last name first). Document
        title. Date of Internet publication. <URL>
        or other retrieval information (Date of
        access).

Internet sources differ in the kinds of information that are important for retrieval, and the model for each type of source reflects the information needed to retrieve that source. For example, for documents that originate as **electronic mail** (including personal email, **newsgroup** and **HyperNews** postings, and **listserv** messages), the author's email address is included after the author's name to help readers authenticate the source. The following models enable you to document Internet sources in a manner consistent with the principles of MLA style.[1]

---

[1]For a discussion on the rationale for these models, see Andrew Harnack and Gene Kleppinger, "Beyond the *MLA Handbook:* Documenting Sources on the Internet" in *Kairos: A Journal for Teaching Writing in Webbed Environments* 1.2 (1996) <http://english .ttu.edu/kairos/1.2/inbox/mla_archive.html>.

1 World Wide Web site

To document a file available for viewing and downloading via the **World Wide Web**, provide the following information:

- author's name (if known)
- title of document, in quotation marks
- title of complete work (if applicable), in italics or underlined
- date of publication or last revision (if known)
- URL, in angle brackets
- date of access, in parentheses

▶ Harris, Jonathan G. "The Return of the Witch Hunts." <u>Witchhunt Information Page</u>. <http://liquid2-sun.mit.edu/fells.short.html> (28 May 1996).

▶ Shade, Leslie R. "Gender Issues in Computer Networking." 1993. <http://www.mit.edu:8001/people/sorokin/women/lrs.html> (28 May 1996).

2 Email message

To document an **email** message, provide the following information:

- author's name (if known)
- author's email address, in angle brackets
- subject line from posting, in quotation marks
- date of publication
- type of communication (personal email, distribution list, office communication)
- date of access, in parentheses

▶ Franke, Norman. <frankel@llnl.gov> "SoundApp 2.0.2." 29 Apr. 1996. Personal email. (3 May 1996).

▶ Robinette, Danny. <robinetted@ccmail.gate.eku.edu> "Epiphany Project." 30 Apr. 1996. Office communication. (29 May 1996).

3 HyperNews posting

To document a **HyperNews** posting, provide the following information:

- author's name
- author's email address, in angle brackets
- subject line or title of posting, in quotation marks
- date of publication
- type of message (if appropriate)
- URL, in angle brackets
- date of access, in parentheses

▶ LaLiberte, Daniel. <liberte@ncsa.uiuc.edu>
        "HyperNews Instructions." 23 May 1996.
        <http://union.ncsa.uiuc.edu/HyperNews/get
        /hypernews/instructions.html> (24 May
        1996).

▶ Saffran, Art. <saffran@wisbar.org> "It's Not
        That Hard." 5 Jan. 1996. Reply to
        "HyperNews Instructions" by Daniel
        LaLiberte. <http://union.ncsa.uiuc.edu
        /HyperNews/get/hypernews/instructions
        /90/1/1.html> (24 May 1996).

4 Listserv message

To document a **listserv** message, provide the following information:

- author's name (if known)
- author's email address, in angle brackets
- subject line from posting, in quotation marks
- date of publication
- address of listserv, in angle brackets
- date of access, in parentheses

▶ Parente, Victor. <vrparent@mailbox.syr.edu> "On
        Expectations of Class Participation." 27
        May 1996. <philosed@sued.syr.edu> (29 May
        1996).

To document a file that can be retrieved from a list's server or Web address, provide the following information after the publication date:

- address of listserv, in angle brackets
- address or URL for list's archive, preceded by *via* and enclosed in angle brackets
- date of access, in parentheses

▶ Carbone, Nick. <nickc@english.umass.edu> "NN
       960126: Followup to Don's Comments about
       Citing URLs." 26 Jan. 1996. <acw-l@unicorn
       .acs.ttu.edu> via <http://www.ttu.edu/lists
       /acw-l> (17 Feb. 1996).

5 Newsgroup message

To document information posted in a **newsgroup** discussion, provide the following information:

- author's name (if known)
- author's email address, in angle brackets
- subject line from posting, in quotation marks
- date of publication
- name of newsgroup, in angle brackets
- date of access, in parentheses

▶ Slade, Robert. <res@maths.bath.ac.uk> "UNIX Made
       Easy." 26 Mar. 1996. <alt.books.reviews>
       (31 Mar. 1996).

If, after following all the suggestions in 4c-3, you cannot determine the author's name, then use the author's email address, enclosed in angle brackets, as the main entry. When you alphabetize such sources in your Works Cited, treat the first letter of the email address as though it were capitalized.

▶ <lrm583@aol.com> "Thinking of Adoption." 26 May
       1996. <alt.adoption> (29 May 1996).

6 Synchronous communication

To document a **synchronous communication**, such as those posted in **MOOs**, **MUDs**, and **IRCs**, provide the following information:

- name of speaker(s) (if known), or name of site
- title of event (if appropriate), in quotation marks
- date of event
- type of communication (group discussion, personal interview), if not indicated elsewhere in entry
- address, using a URL (in angle brackets) or command-line directions
- date of access, in parentheses

▶ LambdaMOO. "Seminar Discussion on Netiquette."
      28 May 1996. <telnet://lambda.parc.xerox
      .edu:8888> (28 May 1996).

▶ Harnack, Andrew. "Words." 4 Apr. 1996. Group
      discussion. telnet moo.du.org/port=8888
      (5 Apr. 1996).

7 Telnet site

To document a **telnet** site or a file available via telnet, provide the following information:

- author's name (if known)
- title of document (if known), in quotation marks
- title of full work (if applicable), in italics or underlined
- date of publication (if available), followed by a period
- word *telnet*
- complete telnet address, with no closing punctuation
- directions for accessing document
- date of access, in parentheses

▶ Aquatic Conservation Network. "About the Aquatic
      Conservation Network." National Capital
      Freenet. telnet freenet.carleton.ca login
      as guest, go acn, press 1 (28 May 1996).

▶ California Department of Pesticide Regulation.
      "Pest Management Information." CSU Fresno
      ATI-NET. telnet caticsuf.csufresno.edu login
      as super, press a, press k (28 May 1996).

8 FTP site

To document a file available for downloading via **file transfer protocol**, provide the following information:

- author's name (if known)
- title of document, in quotation marks
- date of publication (if known)
- abbreviation *ftp*
- address of FTP site, with no closing punctuation
- full path to follow to find document, with no closing punctuation
- date of access, in parentheses

▶ Altar, Ted W. "Vitamin B12 and Vegans." 14 Jan.
      1993. ftp wiretap.spies.com Library
      /Article/Food/b12.txt (28 May 1996).

You can use a URL (enclosed in angle brackets) instead of the command, address, and path elements.

▶ Matloff, Norm. "Immigration Forum." <ftp://
      heather.cs.ucdavis.edu/pub/Immigration
      /Index.html> (28 May 1996).

9 Gopher site

To document information obtained by using the **gopher** search protocol, provide the following information:

- author's name (if known)
- title of document, in quotation marks
- date of publication (if known)
- any print publication information, italicized or under-lined where appropriate
- URL, in angle brackets
- date of access, in parentheses

▶ Smith, Charles A. "National Extension Model of
      Critical Parenting Practices." 1994.
      <gopher://tinman.mes.umn.edu:4242/11/Other
      /Other/NEM_Parent> (28 May 1996).

To document the location of information using a gopher command-path format, give the following information instead of the URL:

- word *gopher*
- site name
- path followed to access document, with slashes to indicate menu selections

▶ "Commons Sense: A Viewer's Guide to the British
    House of Commons." gopher c-span.org
    Transcripts and Publications/C-SPAN
    Publications/Commons Sense (29 May 1996).

10 Linkage data

To document a specific file and give **linkage data** showing its hypertext context, provide the following information:

- author's name (if known)
- title of document, in quotation marks
- abbreviation *Lkd.* ("linked from")
- title of document to which file is linked, in italics or underlined
- additional linkage details (if applicable), preceded by *at*
- date of publication (if known)
- URL for source document, in angle brackets
- date of access, in parentheses

▶ Hoemann, George H. "Electronic Style--Elements of
    Citation." Lkd. <u>Electronic Style Page</u>, at
    "Continue" and "Citation Elements." 3 Nov.
    1995. <http://funnelweb.utcc.utk.edu
    /~hoemann/style.html> (29 May 1996).

▶ Miller, Allison. "Allison Miller's Home Page."
    Lkd. <u>EKU Honors Program Home Page</u>, at
    "Personal Pages." <http://www.csc.eku
    .edu/honors> (2 April 1996).

Work Cited

Gibaldi, Joseph. *MLA Handbook for Writers of Research Papers.*
New York: Modern Language Association, 1995.

CHAPTER SIX

Using APA Style to Cite and Document Sources

The fourth edition of the *Publication Manual of the American Psychological Association* (1994) provides documentation advice for writers in the social sciences. Written primarily for authors preparing manuscripts for professional publication in scholarly journals, the manual discusses manuscript content and organization, writing style, and manuscript preparation. It also offers advice for student writers in an appendix.

The *Publication Manual* instructs writers to document quotations, paraphrases, summaries, and other information from sources as follows: "Document your study throughout the text by citing by author and date the words you researched. This style of citation briefly identifies the source for readers and enables them to locate the source of information in the alphabetical reference list at the end of an article" (p. 168). When using APA style, consult the *Publication Manual* for general style requirements (e.g., style for metric units) and for advice on preparing manuscripts and electronic texts. This chapter follows the conventions of APA citation style.

6a   Adapting APA style to cite Internet sources

Although the *Publication Manual* gives recommendations for citing some kinds of electronic sources (e.g., subscriber-based and general-access online journal articles available via **email** or **FTP**), it acknowledges that "at the time of writing this edition, a standard had not yet emerged for referencing on-line information" (p. 218). Because the manual was published before the development of the **Internet** as we now know it, it does not have guidelines for citing **World Wide Web** sites, **HyperNews** postings, and other Internet sources. The following citation guidelines extend the principles and conventions of APA citation style to Internet sources.[1]

1   Link an in-text citation of an Internet source to a corresponding entry in the References.

In APA style, each text reference is linked to a specific entry in the list of References. The essential elements of an in-text citation are the author's last name (or the document's title, if no author is identified) and the date of publication. Information such as a page or chapter number

> **Box 6.1**
> **Using italics and underlining in APA style**
>
> APA style italicizes certain elements (e.g., book and journal titles) in printed publications but recommends underlining those elements in manuscripts. The use of underlining to represent italics becomes a problem when you compose texts for online publication. On the World Wide Web, underlining in a document indicates that the underlined word or phrase is an active hypertext link. (All HTML editing programs automatically underline any text linked to another hypertext or Web site.)
>
> When composing Web documents, avoid underlining. Instead, use italics for titles, for emphasis, and for words, letters, and numbers referred to as such. When you write with programs such as email that don't allow italics, type an underscore mark _like this_ before and after text you would otherwise italicize or underline.

---

[1]For final copy, the *Publication Manual* specifies the "hanging indent" format for references, with each entry's first line set flush left and subsequent lines indented. Unless your instructor suggests otherwise, it is the format we recommend. Note, however, that for manuscripts being submitted to journals, APA requires the reverse (first lines indented, subsequent lines set flush left), assuming that it will be converted by a typesetting system to a hanging indent.

may be added to show where in a source cited material appears.

Create an in-text reference to an Internet source in text by using a signal phrase, a parenthetical citation, or both a previewing sentence and a parenthetical citation.

Using a signal phrase To introduce a short quotation, paraphrase, or summary, mention the author's name either in an introductory signal phrase or in a parenthetical reference immediately following the signal phrase and containing the publication date. (See 4e for a discussion of signal phrases and verbs.)

signal phrase

▶ Weisenmiller (1995) reports that "the Macintosh Power PC has made a significant impact on the prepress industry of the southeastern United States" (Abstract).

signal phrase

▶ According to one study (Weisenmiller, 1995), a majority of companies have adopted the Macintosh Power into their company's production processes. Investment in Macintosh PowerPCs has generally created new workstations for these companies rather than replacing older workstations (chap. 5).

Here is the References entry for this source:

▶ Weisenmiller, E. M. (1995). The impact of the Macintosh Power PC on the prepress industry of the southeastern United States. <http://teched.vt.edu/ElectronicPortfolios /Weisenmiller.ep/Thesistoc.html> (1996, May 26).

Using a parenthetical citation after cited material Place the author's name and the source's date of publication in parentheses immediately after the end of the cited material.

▶ Many companies have been successful in using the Macintosh Power PC in the prepress process (Weisenmiller, 1995, chap. 5).

Using a previewing sentence and a parenthetical citation
To introduce and identify the source of a long quotation (one comprising 40 or more words), use a previewing sentence that names the author and ends in a colon. By briefly announcing the content of an extended quotation, a previewing sentence tells readers what to look for in the quotation. Indent the block quotation five spaces (or one paragraph indent). At the end of the quotation, after the final punctuation mark, indicate in parentheses any text division that indicates the quotation's location in the source document.

▶ The Librarians Association of the University of Chicago (1996) notes that recent developments in scholarly Internet publication now urge us to rethink the way we give credit to our sources:

> The ease with which authors can broadcast works worldwide through the new media makes understanding of copyright and fair use increasingly important. The ease of making digital recordings and of download-ing works from the Internet does not nec-essarily mean that the information can be adapted or reproduced without permission or royalty payment. Likewise, the lack of a copyright statement does not imply that a work is in the public domain. To avoid infringement of intellectual property rights, educators and students must exer-cise caution in producing their own educa-tional multimedia programs--especially if these are later published on the World-Wide Web. (II.A. Introduction)

Here is the References entry:

▶ Librarians Association of the University of California. (1996, February 1). New hori-zons in scholarly communication: Part 2. New publishing models. <http://www.ucsc .edu/scomm/publishing.html> (1996, May 28).

2 Substitute Internet text divisions for page numbers.

The *Publication Manual* (1994) requires that "[you] give the author, year, and page number in parentheses (paragraph numbers may be used in place of page numbers for electronic text)" when you use a direct quotation (p. 97). Because Internet sources are rarely marked with page numbers, you will not always be able show exactly where cited material comes from. If a source has internal divisions, use these instead of page numbers in your citation. Be sure to use divisions inherent in the document and not those provided by your browsing software.

▶ J. McGann (1996, May 6) believes that even decentered hypertexts are nevertheless always ordered: "To say that a HyperText is not centrally organized does not mean--at least does not mean to me--that the HyperText structure has no governing order(s), even at a theoretical level" (Coda: A Note on the Decentered Text).

Here is the References entry:

▶ McGann, J. (1996, May 6). The rationale of HyperText. <http://jefferson.village.virginia.edu/public/jjm2f/rationale.html> (1996, May 27).

3 Use source-reflective statements to show where cited material ends.

Many Internet sources appear as single screens. To let your readers know where your use of a single-screen Internet source with no text divisions ends, use a source-reflective statement.

Source-reflective statements give you an opportunity to assert your authorial voice. Writers use source-reflective statements to provide editorial comment, clarification, qualification, amplification, dissent, agreement, and so on. In the following example, the absence of a source-reflective statement creates uncertainty as to whether the

writer has finished citing an Internet source or has mere-
ly moved from quoting directly to paraphrasing.

▶ Mike Sosteric observes that "in recent years,
  scholarly communication has virtually exploded
  into the on-line electronic world [and] this
  has brought a number of demonstrable benefits
  to the scholarly communication process." We can
  expect many more electronic journals to appear
  online in the next few years--surely a benefit
  to scholarly communications.

In the next example, the writer has added a source-reflective statement to show that use of the source has ended.

▶ Mike Sosteric observes that "in recent years,
  scholarly communication has virtually exploded
  into the on-line electronic world [and] this
  has brought a number of demonstrable benefits
  to the scholarly communication process."
  ⌐⌐ Sosteric's observation means that we can expect
  │ many more electronic journals to appear online
  │ in the next few years--surely a benefit to
  │ scholarly communications.
  └────────────────── **source-reflective statement**

Here is the References entry:

▶ Sosteric, M. (1996). Electronic journals and
    scholarly communication: Notes and issues.
    <u>Electronic Journal of Sociology</u> <http://
    129.128.113.200:8010/vol002.001/Sosteric
    -Abstract.html> (1996, October 21).

6b References

When using APA style, place a list of cited sources,
arranged alphabetically, after the text of your essay but
before any appendixes or explanatory notes. The
Publication Manual (1994) gives the following general
models for References entries:

Book

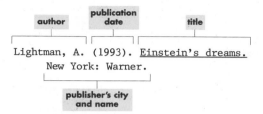

```
Lightman, A. (1993). Einstein's dreams.
     New York: Warner.
```

Periodical article

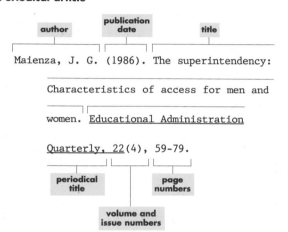

```
Maienza, J. G. (1986). The superintendency:

Characteristics of access for men and

women. Educational Administration

Quarterly, 22(4), 59-79.
```

The *Publication Manual* also presents numerous variations that accommodate a variety of print sources (e.g., translation, government document). For detailed information on creating a References list, see Chapter 3 of the *Publication Manual,* "APA Editorial Style."

Extending the citation practice of the *Publication Manual* to include Internet sources produces the following model:

Online document

▶ Author's name (last name, first and any middle initials). (Date of Internet publication). Document title. <URL> or other retrieval information (Date of access).

Box 6.2
Using hypertext to document sources on the Web

The hypertext environment of the World Wide Web doesn't just alter the way you do research, it also lets you document sources in a new way—by using hypertext links. Electronic journals published on the Web are already replacing traditional notes, References listings, appendixes, and other supporting text with links to the documents being cited. To read more about hypertext documentation, see 10f in this book. For an example of how it works, look at the format of *Electronic Journal of Sociology* at <http://129.128.113.200:8010>.

Internet sources differ in the kinds of information that are important for retrieval, and the model for each type of source reflects the information needed to retrieve that source. For example, for documents that originated as electronic mail (including personal email, newsgroup and HyperNews postings, and listserv messages), the author's email address is included after the author's name to help readers authenticate the source. The following models enable you to document Internet sources in a manner consistent with the principles of APA style.[2]

1 World Wide Web site

To document a file available for viewing and downloading via the **World Wide Web**, provide the following information:

- author's name (if known)
- date of publication or last revision (if known), in parentheses
- title of document
- title of complete work (if applicable), underlined
- URL, in angle brackets
- date of access, in parentheses

---

[2]These documentation models are much more compact than those suggested by others (Land, 1995; Li & Crane, 1993, 1996). The preliminary models in the *Publication Manual,* drawn from Li and Crane (1993), include descriptive expressions such as "[On-line]," "Available:," and "Hostname:," which are not necessary for understanding Internet specifications and also place potentially misleading symbols near electronic addresses.

▶ Harris, J. G. (n.d.). The return of the witch
    hunts. <u>Witchhunt Information Page.</u>
    <http://liquid2-sun.mit.edu/fells
    .short.html> (1996, May 28).

▶ Shade, L. R. (1993). Gender issues in computer
    networking. <http://www.mit.edu:8001
    /people/sorokin/women/lrs.html>
    (1996, May 28).

2 Email message

The *Publication Manual* categorizes all **electronic mail** as a
form of personal communication that does not provide
"recoverable data." The *Manual* advises against including
personal communications in the References and suggests
citing them only in the text. Many writers, however, consider it good practice to list email messages in the
References, especially when a message's content is
scholarly.

To document an email message, provide the following
information:

* author's name (if known)
* author's email address, in angle brackets
* date of publication, in parentheses
* subject line from posting
* type of communication (personal email, distribution
  list, office communication), in square brackets
* date of access, in parentheses

▶ Franke, N. <frankel@llnl.gov> (1996, April 29).
    SoundApp 2.0.2 [Personal email]. (1996,
    May 3).

▶ Robinette, D. <robinetted@ccmail.gate.eku.edu>
    (1996, April 30). Epiphany project [Office
    communication]. (1996, May 23).

3 HyperNews posting

To document a **HyperNews** posting, provide the following information:

* author's name
* author's email address, in angle brackets

- date of publication, in parentheses
- subject line or title of posting
- type of message (if appropriate), in square brackets
- URL, in angle brackets
- date of access, in parentheses

▶ LaLiberte, D. <liberte@ncsa.uiuc.edu> (1996, May
    23). HyperNews instructions. <http://union
    .ncsa.uiuc.edu/HyperNews/get/hypernews
    /instructions.html> (1996, May 24).

▶ Saffran, A. <saffran@wisbar.org> (1996, January
    5). It's not that hard [Reply to HyperNews
    instructions, by D. LaLiberte]. <http://
    union.ncsa.uiuc.edu/HyperNews/get/hypernews
    /instructions/90/1/1.html> (1996, May 24).

4 Listserv message

To document a **listserv** message, provide the following
information:

- author's name (if known)
- author's email address, in angle brackets
- date of publication, in parentheses
- subject line from posting
- address of listserv, in angle brackets
- date of access, in parentheses

▶ Parente, V. <vrparent@mailbox.syr.edu> (1996,
    May 27). On expectations of class partici-
    pation. <philosed@sued.syr.edu> (1996,
    May 29).

To document a file that can be retrieved from a list's
server or Web address, provide the following information
after the publication date:

- address of listserv, in angle brackets
- address or URL for list's archive, preceded by *via* and
  enclosed in angle brackets
- date of access, in parentheses

▶ Carbone, N. <nickc@english.umass.edu> (1996,
     January 26). NN 960126: Followup to Don's
     comments about citing URLs. <acw-1@uni
     corn.acs.ttu.edu> via <http://www.ttu
     .edu/lists/acw-1> (1996, February 17).

5 Newsgroup message

To document information posted in a **newsgroup** discussion, provide the following information:

- author's name (if known)
- author's email address, in angle brackets
- date of publication, in parentheses
- subject line from posting
- name of newsgroup, in angle brackets
- date of access, in parentheses

▶ Slade, R. <res@maths.bath.ac.uk> (1996, March
     26). UNIX made easy. <alt.books.reviews>
     (1996, March 31).

If, after following all the suggestions in 4c-3, you cannot determine the author's name, then use the author's email address, enclosed in angle brackets, as the main entry. When you alphabetize such sources in your References, treat the first letter of the email address as though it were capitalized.

▶ <lrm583@aol.com> (1996, May 26). Thinking of
     adoption. <alt.adoption> (1996, May 29).

6 Synchronous communication

To document a **synchronous communication**, such as those posted in **MOOs**, **MUDs**, and **IRCs**, provide the following information:

- name of speaker(s) (if known), or name of site
- date of event, in parentheses
- title of event (if appropriate)
- type of communication (group discussion, personal

interview), if not indicated elsewhere in entry, in
square brackets
- address, using a URL (in angle brackets) or command-
line directions
- date of access, in parentheses

▶ LambdaMOO. (1996, May 28). Seminar discussion
on netiquette. <telnet://lambda.parc
.xerox.edu:8888> (1996, May 28).

▶ Harnack, A. (1996, April 4). Words. [Group dis-
cussion]. telnet moo.du.org/port=8888
(1996, April 5).

7 Telnet site

To document a **telnet** site or a file available via telnet, provide the following information:

- author's name (if known)
- date of publication (if known), in parentheses
- title of document (if known)
- title of full work (if applicable), underlined
- word *telnet*
- complete telnet address, with no closing punctuation
- directions for accessing document
- date of access, in parentheses

▶ Aquatic Conservation Network. (n.d.). About the
Aquatic Conservation Network. National
Capital Freenet. telnet freenet.carleton
.ca login as guest, go acn, press 1
(1996, May 28).

▶ California Department of Pesticide Regulation.
(n.d.). Pest management information. CSU
Fresno ATI-NET. telnet caticsuf.csufres
no.edu login as super, press a, press k
(1996, May 28).

8 FTP site

To document a file available for downloading via **file
transfer protocol**, provide the following information:

- author's name (if known)
- date of publication (if known), in parentheses
- title of document
- abbreviation *ftp*
- address of FTP site, with no closing punctuation
- full path to follow to find document, with no closing punctuation
- date of access, in parentheses

▶ Altar, T. W. (1993, January 14). Vitamin
B12 and vegans. ftp wiretap.spies.com
Library/Article/Food/b12.txt (1996, May
28).

You can use a URL (enclosed in angle brackets) instead of the command, address, and path elements.

▶ Matloff, N. (n.d.). Immigration forum. <ftp://
heather.cs.ucdavis.edu/pub/Immigration
/Index.html> (1996, May 28).

9 Gopher site

To document information obtained by using the **gopher** search protocol, provide the following information:

- author's name (if known)
- date of publication, in parentheses
- title of document
- any print publication information, underlined where appropriate
- URL, in angle brackets
- date of access, in parentheses

▶ Smith, C. A. (1994). National extension model
of critical parenting practices. <gopher://
tinman.mes.umn.edu:4242/11/Other/Other
/NEM_Parent> (1996, May 28).

To document the location of information using a gopher command-path format, give the following information instead of the URL:

- word *gopher*
- site name
- path followed to access document, with slashes to indicate menu selections

▶ Commons sense: A viewer's guide to the British House of Commons. (n.d.). gopher c-span .org Transcripts and Publications/C-SPAN Publications/Commons Sense (1996, May 29).

10 Linkage data

To document a specific file and give **linkage data** showing its hypertext context, provide the following information:

- author's name (if known)
- date of publication (if known), in parentheses
- title of document
- abbreviation *Lkd.* ("linked from")
- title of document to which file is linked, underlined
- additional linkage details (if applicable), preceded by *at*
- URL for source document, in angle brackets
- date of access, in parentheses

▶ Hoemann, G. H. (1995, November 3). Electronic style--elements of citation. Lkd. <u>Electronic Style Page,</u> at "Continue" and "Citation Elements." <http://funnelweb .utcc.utk.edu/~hoemann/style.html> (1996, May 29).

▶ Miller, A. (n.d.). Allison Miller's home page. Lkd. <u>EKU Honors Program Home Page,</u> at "Personal Pages." <http://www.csc.eku .edu/honors> (1996, April 2).

Reference

American Psychological Association. (1995). *Publication Manual of the American Psychological Association* (4th ed.). Washington, DC: American Psychological Association.

CHAPTER SEVEN

Using *Chicago* Style to Cite and Document Sources

This chapter's guidelines for citing Internet sources are based on the principles presented in the fourteenth edition of *The Chicago Manual of Style*.[1] The *Chicago Manual* offers two documentation styles, one using notes and bibliographies, the other using author-date citations and lists of references. The *Chicago Manual* also gives guidelines for spelling and punctuation and discusses the treatment of numbers, quotations, illustrations, tables, foreign languages, mathematical symbols, abbreviations, and so on.

To mark citations in the text, the *Chicago Manual*'s note-bibliography style places a superscript number after each quotation, paraphrase, or summary. Citations are numbered sequentially throughout the text, and each citation corresponds to a numbered note containing publication information about the source cited. Such notes are called *footnotes* when printed at the foot of a page and *endnotes* when printed at the end of an essay, chapter, or book. These notes generally serve two purposes: to cite sources and to make cross-references to previous notes. This chapter follows the conventions of the *Chicago Manual*'s note-bibliography style.

---

[1] *The Chicago Manual of Style*, 14th ed. (Chicago: University of Chicago Press, 1993). When this chapter cites the *Chicago Manual*, it does so in footnotes such as this one.

7a Adapting *Chicago* style to cite Internet sources

Although the *Chicago Manual* provides some advice for documenting information from computerized data services, computer programs, and electronic documents, it contains no advice on documenting Internet sources. The following recommendations adapt the *Chicago Manual*'s guidelines and models to Internet sources.

1 Introduce the source of a short quotation, paraphrase, or summary by using either a signal phrase set off by a comma or a signal verb with a *that* clause.

The following two examples show how signal phrases can be used to introduce cited material. (See 4e for a discussion of signal phrases and verbs.)

signal phrase

▶ According to Brendan P. Kehoe, "We are truly in an information society. Now more than ever, moving vast amounts of information quickly across great distances is one of our most pressing needs."[1]

signal phrase

▶ Brendan P. Kehoe reminds us that "we are truly in an information society. Now more than ever, moving vast amounts of information quickly across great distances is one of our most pressing needs."[1]

Here is the note for this source:

▶   1. Brendan P. Kehoe, <u>Zen and the Art of the Internet,</u> January 1992, <http://freenet.buffa lo.edu/~popmusic/zen10.txt> (4 June 1996), Network Basics.

Box 7.1
Using italics and underlining in *Chicago* style

Chicago style recommends italicizing certain elements (e.g., book and journal titles) in printed text. Use underlining if your instructor requires it or if your typewriter or wordprocessing program can't produce italics. However, the use of underlining to represent italics becomes a problem when you compose texts for online publication. On the World Wide Web, underlining in a document indicates that the underlined word or phrase is an active hypertext link. (All HTML editing programs automatically underline any text linked to another hypertext or Web site.)

When composing Web documents, avoid underlining. Instead, use italics for titles, for emphasis, and for words, letters, and numbers referred to as such. When you write with programs such as email that don't allow italics, type an underscore mark _like this_ before and after text you would otherwise italicize or underline.

---

2 Link an in-text citation of an Internet source to a corresponding note.

According to *Chicago* style, the first note for a given source should include all the information necessary to identify and locate the source: the author's full name, the full title of the book, the name of the editor, the place of publication, the name of the publisher, the publication date, and page numbers indicating the location of the quoted information. In subsequent references to the source, give only the author's last name followed by a comma, a shortened version of the title followed by a comma, and the page reference.

Indent the first line of each note five spaces (or one paragraph indent). Begin with a number followed by a period. Leave one space before the first word of the note. If you are double-spacing your manuscript, double-space the notes as well.

Book (first note)

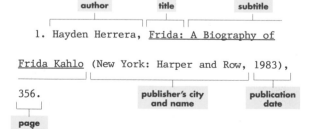

1. Hayden Herrera, <u>Frida: A Biography of Frida Kahlo</u> (New York: Harper and Row, 1983), 356.

Book (subsequent note)

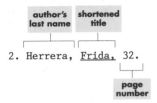

```
2. Herrera, Frida, 32.
```

Periodical article (first note)

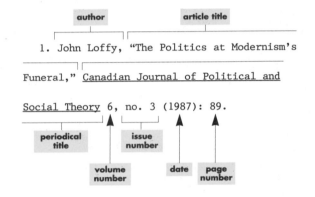

```
1. John Loffy, "The Politics at Modernism's

Funeral," Canadian Journal of Political and

Social Theory 6, no. 3 (1987): 89.
```

Periodical article (subsequent note)

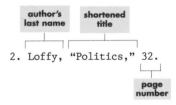

```
2. Loffy, "Politics," 32.
```

Here is how you would document the first reference to a source:

▶ According to Professor Tom Wilson, "the idea of the electronic library has emerged as a model for future systems, already implemented in some forms and to some degree in various places."[1]

Here is the corresponding note:

▶ 1. Tom Wilson, 'In the Beginning Was the
Word': Social and Economic Factors in Scholarly
Electronic Communication," ELVIRA Conference
Keynote Paper, 1009, 10 April 1995, <http://
www2.shef.ac.uk/infor_studies/lecturer/elvira
.html> (23 May 1996), Introduction.

Here is a second reference to the source:

▶ Professor Wilson contends that "a new system of
scholarly communication, based on electronic
systems and networks, not only necessitates new
models for the concepts of journals, library,
and publishing, but also new interpersonal and
institutional mores, customs, and practices."[2]

Here is the note:

▶ 2. Wilson, "In the Beginning," Introduction.

3 Substitute Internet text divisions for page numbers.

The *Chicago Manual* requires that a note include a page
reference or similar information for locating material in a
source. Because Internet sources are rarely marked with
page numbers, you will not always be able to show exactly
where cited material comes from. If a source has internal
divisions, use these instead of page numbers in your citation. Be sure to use divisions inherent in the document
and not those provided by your browsing software.

In the following example, the Introduction serves as a
text division for an Internet source.

▶ As TyAnna Herrington observes, "Nicholas
Negroponte's <u>Being Digital</u> provides another welcome not only into an age of technological
ubiquity, but into a way of 'being' with technology."[1]

Here is the note:

▶ 1. TyAnna K. Herrington, "Being Is
Believing," review of <u>Being Digital,</u> by
Nicholas Negroponte, <u>Kairos: A Journal for
Teaching Writing in Webbed Environments</u> 1.1

> **Box 7.2**
> **Using hypertext to document sources on the Web**
>
> The hypertext environment of the World Wide Web doesn't just
> alter the way you do research, it also lets you document sources
> in a new way—by using hypertext links. Electronic journals pub-
> lished on the Web are already replacing traditional notes, bibli-
> ographies, appendixes, and other supporting text with links to the
> documents being cited. To read more about hypertext documenta-
> tion, see 10f in this book. For an example of how it works, look at
> the format of the *Harvard Educational Review* at <http://hugse1
> .harvard.edu/~hepg/her.html>.

```
(1996), <http://english.ttu.edu/kairos/1.1> (24
May 1996), Introduction.
```

7b Notes

See 7a-2 for the basic *Chicago*-style models for documenting printed books and periodicals. For additional information about documenting print sources, see Chapters 15
and 16 of the *Chicago Manual*.

Extending the citation practice of the *Chicago Manual*
to include Internet sources produces the following model:

▶   1. Author's name (in normal order), document
    title, date of Internet publication, <URL> or
    other retrieval information (date of access),
    text division (if applicable).

This model combines the stylistic elements of *Chicago*-
style author-date citation[2] with the elements necessary for
identifying an Internet source. The publication date
appears close to the title of the document, while the date
of access follows the **URL** or other access information.
The text division occupies the final position in the note, as
page numbers would for a printed source.

Internet sources differ in the kinds of information
that are important for retrieval, and the model for each
type of source reflects the information needed to retrieve
that source. For example, for documents that originated
as **electronic mail** (including personal email, **newsgroup** and **HyperNews** postings, and **listserv** messages), the author's email address is included after the
author's name to help readers authenticate the source.

---

[2]See *Chicago Manual,* sections 15.154 and 15.231.

The following models enable you to document Internet sources in a manner consistent with the principles of *Chicago* style.

1 World Wide Web site

To document a file available for viewing and download-ing via the **World Wide Web**, provide the following information:

- author's name (if known)
- title of document, in quotation marks
- title of complete work (if applicable), in italics or underlined
- date of publication or last revision (if known) (other-wise use *n.d.*)
- URL, in angle brackets
- date of access, in parentheses

▶ 1. Jonathan G. Harris, "The Return of the Witch Hunts," <u>Witchhunt Information Page,</u> n.d., <http://liquid2-sun.mit.edu/fells.short.html> (28 May 1996).

▶ 2. Leslie R. Shade, "Gender Issues in Computer Networking," 1993, <http://www.mit .edu:8001/people/sorokin/women/lrs.html> (28 May 1996).

2 Email message

To document an **email** message, provide the following information:

- author's name (if known)
- author's email address, in angle brackets
- subject line from posting, in quotation marks
- date of publication
- type of communication (personal email, distribution list, office communication)
- date of access, in parentheses

▶ 1. Norman Franke, <frankel@llnl.gov> "SoundApp 2.0.2," 29 April 1996, personal email (3 May 1996).

▶ 2. Danny Robinette, <robinetted@ccmail .gate.eku.edu> "Epiphany Project," 30 April 1996, office communication (29 May 1996).

3 HyperNews posting

To document a HyperNews posting, provide the following information:

- author's name
- author's email address, in angle brackets
- subject line or title of posting, in quotation marks
- date of publication
- type of message (if appropriate)
- URL, in angle brackets
- date of access, in parentheses

▶ 1. Daniel LaLiberte, <liberte@ncsa.uiuc.edu> "HyperNews Instructions," 23 May 1996, <http://union.ncsa.uiuc.edu/HyperNews/get/hypernews/instructions.html> (24 May 1996).

▶ 2. Art Saffran, "It's Not That Hard," <saffran@wisbar.org> 5 January 1996, reply to "HyperNews Instructions" by Daniel LaLiberte, <http://union.ncsa.uiuc.edu/HyperNews/get/hypernews/instructions/90/1/1.html> (24 May 1996).

4 Listserv message

To document a listserv message, provide the following information:

- author's name (if known)
- author's email address, in angle brackets
- subject line from posting, in quotation marks
- date of publication
- address of listserv, in angle brackets
- date of access, in parentheses

▶   1. Victor Parente, <vrparent@mailbox.syr.edu>
"On Expectations of Class Participation," 27
May 1996, <philosed@sued.syr.edu> (29 May 1996).

To document a file that can be retrieved from a list's
server or Web address, provide the following information
after the publication date:

- address of listserv, in angle brackets
- address or URL for list's archive, preceded by *via* and
  enclosed in angle brackets
- date of access, in parentheses

▶   1. Nick Carbone, <nickc@english.umass.edu>
"NN 960126: Followup to Don's Comments about
Citing URLs," 26 January 1996, <acw-l@unicorn
.acs.ttu.edu> via <http://www.ttu.edu/lists
/acw-l> (17 February 1996).

5 Newsgroup message

To document information posted in a **newsgroup** discussion, provide the following information:

- author's name (if known)
- author's email address, in angle brackets
- subject line from posting, in quotation marks
- date of publication
- name of newsgroup, in angle brackets
- date of access, in parentheses

▶   1. Robert Slade, <res@maths.bath.ac.uk> "UNIX
Made Easy," 26 March 1996, <alt.books.reviews>
(31 March 1996).

If, after following all the suggestions in 4c-3, you cannot
determine the author's name, then use the author's email
address, enclosed in angle brackets, as the main entry.
When you alphabetize such sources in your Bibliography,
treat the first letter of the email address as though it were
capitalized.

▶   2. <lrm583@aol.com> "Thinking of Adoption,"
26 May 1996, <alt.adoption> (29 May 1996).

6 Synchronous communication

To document a **synchronous communication**, such as those posted in **MOOs**, **MUDs**, and **IRCs**, provide the following information:

- name of speaker(s) (if known), or name of site
- title of event (if appropriate), in quotation marks
- date of event
- type of communication (group discussion, personal interview), if not indicated elsewhere in entry
- address, using a URL (in angle brackets) or command-line directions
- date of access, in parentheses

▶   1. LambdaMOO, "Seminar Discussion on Netiquette," 28 May 1996, <telnet://lambda.parc .xerox.edu:8888> (28 May 1996).

▶   2. Andrew Harnack, "Words," Group Discussion, 4 April 1996, telnet moo.du.org/port=8888 (5 April 1996).

7 Telnet site

To document a **telnet** site or a file available via telnet, provide the following information:

- author's name (if known)
- title of document (if known), in quotation marks
- title of full work (if applicable), in italics or underlined
- date of publication (if available), followed by a period
- word *telnet*
- complete telnet address, with no closing punctuation
- directions for accessing document
- date of access, in parentheses

▶   1. Aquatic Conservation Network, "About the Aquatic Conservation Network," National Capital Freenet, n.d., telnet freenet.carleton.ca login as guest, go acn, press 1 (28 May 1996).

▶ 2. California Department of Pesticide Regulation, "Pest Management Information," <u>CSU Fresno ATI-NET</u>, n.d., telnet caticsuf.csufres no.edu login as super, press a, press k (28 May 1996).

8 FTP site

To document a file for downloading via **file transfer protocol**, provide the following information:

- author's name (if known)
- title of document, in quotation marks
- date of publication (if known)
- abbreviation *ftp*
- address of FTP site, with no closing punctuation
- full path to follow to find document, with no closing punctuation
- date of access, in parentheses

▶ 1. Ted W. Altar, "Vitamin B12 and Vegans," 14 January 1993, ftp wiretap.spies.com Library/Article/Food/b12.txt (28 May 1996).

You can use a URL (enclosed in angle brackets) instead of the command, address, and path elements.

▶ 2. Norm Matloff, "Immigration Forum," n.d., <ftp://heather.cs.ucdavis.edu/pub/Immigration/In dex.html> (28 May 1996).

9 Gopher site

To document information obtained by using the **gopher** search protocol, provide the following information:

- author's name (if known)
- title of document, in quotation marks
- any print publication information, italicized or underlined where appropriate
- URL, in angle brackets
- date of access, in parentheses

▶ 1. Charles A. Smith, "National Extension Model of Critical Parenting Practices," 1994, <gopher://tinman.mes.umn.edu:4242/11/Other/Other/NEM_Parent> (28 May 1996).

To document the location of information using a gopher command-path format, give the following information instead of the URL:

- word *gopher*
- site name
- path followed to access document, with slashes to indicate menu selections

▶ 2. "Commons Sense: A Viewer's Guide to the British House of Commons," n.d., gopher c-span .org Transcripts and Publications/C-SPAN Publications/Commons Sense (29 May 1996).

10 Linkage data

To document a specific file and give **linkage data** showing its hypertext context, provide the following information:

- author's name (if known)
- title of document
- abbreviation *lkd.* ("linked from")
- title of document to which file is linked, in italics or underlined
- additional linkage information (if applicable), preceded by *at*
- date of publication (if known)
- URL for source document, in angle brackets
- date of access, in parentheses

▶ 1. George H. Hoemann, "Electronic Style-- Elements of Citation," lkd. <u>Electronic Style Page,</u> at "Continue" and "Citation Elements," 3 November 1995, <http://funnelweb.utcc.utk.edu /~hoemann/style.html> (29 May 1996).

▶ 2. Allison Miller, "Allison Miller's Home
Page," lkd. <u>EKU Honors Program Home Page,</u> at
"Personal Pages," n.d., <http://www.csc.eku.edu
/honors> (2 April 1996).

7c Bibliography

Since the first note reference to a source includes all the
information necessary to verify or retrieve a citation, your
Chicago-style research paper may not include a
Bibliography. If you decide to include one (or are required
to do so by an instructor or editor), an alphabetized list of
sources will do the trick. (The Bibliography may also be
titled Sources Consulted, Works Cited, or Selected
Bibliography, if any of those titles more accurately
describes the list.)

Bibliography entries differ from first note references in
the following ways:

1. Authors' names are inverted.
2. Elements of entries are separated by periods.
3. The first line of each entry is flush with the left margin, and subsequent lines are indented three or four
   spaces.

If the rest of your manuscript is typed double-spaced,
double-space the Bibliography as well.

Compare the following note with the corresponding
Bibliography entry:

▶ 1. George H. Hoemann, "Electronic Style--
Elements of Citation," lkd. <u>Electronic Style
Page,</u> at "Continue" and "Citation Elements,"
3 November 1995, <http://funnelweb.utcc.utk.edu
/~hoemann/style.html> (29 May 1996).

▶ Hoemann, George H. "Electronic Style--Elements
of Citation." Lkd. <u>Electronic Style Page,</u> at
"Continue" and "Citation Elements." 3
November 1995. <http://funnelweb.utcc.utk.edu
/~hoemann/style.html> (29 May 1996).

CHAPTER EIGHT

Using CBE Style to Cite and Document Sources

This chapter's guidelines for citing Internet sources stem from the principles presented in the sixth edition of *Scientific Style and Format: The CBE Manual for Authors, Editors, and Publishers,* published by the Council of Biology Editors in 1994. Many writers in the natural sciences use the citation style recommended in the *CBE Manual,* which also gives advice for styling and formatting scientific papers, journals, and books for publication. Its editors offer two methods for citing and documenting sources: the citation-sequence system and the name-year system.

8a Using CBE in-text citation style

This section briefly describes the citation-sequence and name-year citation systems. Use the system preferred by your instructor or by the journal you are writing for, and consult Chapter 30 of the *CBE Manual,* "Citations and References," for detailed advice. The Internet documentation models presented in 8b are compatible with the principles of both systems.

> **Box 8.1**
> **Using italics and underlining in CBE style**
>
> CBE style doesn't specify the use of italics or underlining in
> References entries, leaving such matters to the discretion of writers
> and editors. In your writing, you may decide that you need to
> highlight certain titles, terms, or symbols. The use of underlining to
> represent italics becomes a problem when you compose texts for
> online publication. On the World Wide Web, underlining in a
> document indicates that the underlined word or phrase is an
> active hypertext link. (All HTML editing programs automatically
> underline any text linked to another hypertext or Web site.)
>
> When composing Web documents, avoid underlining. Instead,
> use italics for titles, for emphasis, and for words, letters, and num-
> bers referred to as such. When you write with programs such as
> email that don't allow italics, type an underscore mark _like this_
> before and after text you would otherwise italicize or underline.

1 The citation-sequence system

When using the citation-sequence system, key cited
sources to a list of references that are numbered in the
order in which they appear in the text. Use a superscript
number[1] or a number in parentheses (1) following any
reference to a source. (Most instructors prefer superscript
numbers to numbers in parentheses. If you're a student,
ask your instructor which style he or she prefers.) If a single reference points to more than one source, list the
source numbers[1,3,6] in a series. Use a comma (but no following space) to separate two numbers, or numbers[1,3]
that do not form a sequence. Use a dash to separate more
than two numbers[1–3] that form a sequence. If you cite a
source again later in the paper, refer to it by its original
number.

In the citation-sequence format, the date of publication
is listed after the publisher's name (for books) or after the
periodical name (for articles). The following example
uses the citation-sequence system.

▶ Ungvarski[1] claims that most HIV-positive
patients lose weight as their illness progress-
es. The World Health Organization has recog-
nized HIV wasting syndrome as an AIDS-defining
condition.[2]

> HIV wasting is caused partly by an increase in
> the level of tumor necrosis factor (TNF). . . .
> This increase in TNF leads to the accelerated
> muscle breakdown characteristic of HIV wasting
> syndrome.[1,3]

Here are the References entries for these three sources:

▶ [1]Ungvarski PJ, Staats J. HIV/AIDS: A guide to
  nursing care. 3rd ed. Philadelphia: WB Saunders;
  1995. p 47.
  [2]World Health Organization. World health statistics annual: 1993. Geneva: World Health
  Organization; 1994.
  [3]Coodley GO, Loveless MO, Merrill TM. The HIV
  wasting syndrome: a review. J Acquired Immune
  Deficiency Syndromes 1994 July;7(7):681–94.
  p 681.

2 The name-year system

When using the name-year system, key cited sources to
an alphabetically arranged list of references. In the name-
year format, the date of publication immediately follows
the author's name. The following example uses the name-
year system.

▶ The discovery in normal cells of genes capable
  of causing tumors can be considered a milestone
  in cancer research (Stehelin and others 1976).
  Recent work (Sarkar, Zhao, and Sarkar 1995) has
  confirmed the importance of this finding. As
  Bishop and Varmus (1985) point out, numerous
  results now suggest that changes in these genes
  transform normal cells into cancerous ones.

Here are the References entries for these three sources:

▶ Bishop JM, Varmus HE. 1985. Functions and
    origins of retroviral transforming genes.
    In: Weiss R, Teich N, Varmus HE, Coffin J,
    editors. RNA tumor viruses. Cold Spring
    Harbor, NY: Cold Spring Harbor Laboratory
    Press. p 999–1019.

▶ Sarkar T, Zhao W, Sarkar NH. 1995 Oct.
 Expression of jun oncogene in rodent
 and human breast tumors. World Wide Web J
 Biology 1(1). <http://www.epress.com
 /w3jbio/wj6.html> Accessed 1996 23 Oct.

▶ Stehelin D, Varmus HE, Bishop JM, Vogt PK.
 1976. DNA related to the transforming gene(s)
 of avian sarcoma viruses is present in normal
 avian DNA. Nature 260:170–73.

8b   References

The *CBE Manual* provides models for documenting electronic journal articles and books, some of which are available on the **World Wide Web** and by **FTP** and **gopher**. The Council of Biology Editors has established conventions for citing electronically published articles and books, and you are encouraged to follow them as outlined in the *CBE Manual*. When you cite other Internet sources, use the guidelines in this section. The examples shown follow the citation-sequence system, but you can easily adapt them to the name-year system by deleting the superscripts and alphabetizing the entries.

List the References at the end of your research paper but before any appendixes or explanatory notes. For Internet sources, use the following model:

▶ Author's name (last name, first and any middle
 initials). Date of Internet publication.
 Document title. <URL> or other retrieval information. Date of access.

Box 8.2
Using hypertext to document sources on the Web

The hypertext environment of the World Wide Web doesn't just alter the way you do research, it also lets you document sources in a new way—by using hypertext links. Electronic journals published on the Web are already replacing traditional notes, References listings, appendixes, and other supporting text with links to the documents being cited. To read more about hypertext documentation, see 10f in this book. For an example of how it works, look at the format of *The World Wide Web Journal of Biology* at <http://epress.com/w3jbio>.

Internet sources differ in the kinds of information that are important for retrieval, and the model for each type of source reflects the information needed to retrieve that source. For example, for documents that originated as **electronic mail** (including personal email, **newsgroup** and **HyperNews** postings, and **listserv** messages), the author's email address is included after the author's name to help readers authenticate the source. The following models enable you to document Internet sources in a manner consistent with the principles of CBE style.

1 World Wide Web site

To document a file available for viewing and downloading via the **World Wide Web**, provide the following information:

- author's name (if known)
- date of publication or last revision (if known)
- title of document
- title of complete work (if applicable)
- URL, in angle brackets
- date of access

▶ [1]Tardent P. 1995 Nov. Cell biology, annual report 1994. <http://www.unizh.ch/~zool/depts /cell/report94.html> Accessed 1996 Jun 18.

▶ [2]Glockle WG, Nonnenmacher TF. 1995. A fractional calculus approach to self-similar protein dynamics. Biophysical J Abstr 68(1):46. <http:// biosci.cbs.umn.edu/biophys/bj/df-html/df95 /jan95.html#NN> Accessed 1996 Jul 25.

2 Email message

To document an **email** message, provide the following information:

- author's name (if known)
- author's email address, in angle brackets
- date of publication
- subject line from posting

- type of communication (personal email, distribution list, office communication), in square brackets
- date of access

▶ [1]Franke N. <frankel@llnl.gov> 1996 Apr 29.
SoundApp 2.0.2 [Personal email]. Accessed 1996
May 3.

▶ [2]Robinette D. <robinetted@ccmail.gate.eku.edu>
1996 Apr 30. Epiphany project [Office communication]. Accessed 1996 May 23.

3 HyperNews posting

To document a **HyperNews** posting, provide the following information:

- author's name
- author's email address, in angle brackets
- date of publication
- subject line or title of posting
- type of message (if appropriate), in square brackets
- URL, in angle brackets
- date of access

▶ [1]LaLiberte D. <liberte@ncsa.uiuc.edu> 1996 May
23. HyperNews instructions. <http://union.ncsa
.uiuc.edu/HyperNews/get/hypernews/instructions
.html> Accessed 1996 May 24.

▶ [2]Saffran A. <saffran@wisbar.org> 1996 Jan 5.
It's not that hard [Reply to HyperNews instructions, by D. Liberte]. <http://union.ncsa.uiuc
.edu/HyperNews/get/hypernews/instructions
/90/1/1.html> Accessed 1996 May 24.

4 Listserv message

To document a **listserv** message, provide the following information:

- author's name (if known)
- author's email address, in angle brackets
- date of publication

- subject line from posting
- address of listserv, in angle brackets
- date of access

▶ ¹Parente V. <vrparent@mailbox.syr.edu> 1996 May
  27. On expectations of class participation.
  <philosed@sued.syr.edu> Accessed 1996 May 29.

To document a file that can be retrieved from a list's
server or Web address, provide the following information
after the publication date:

- address of listserv, in angle brackets
- address or URL for list's archive, preceded by *via* and
  enclosed in angle brackets
- date of access

▶ ²Carbone N. <nickc@english.umass.edu> 1996 Jan
  26. NN 960126: followup to Don's comments about
  citing URLs. <acw-l@unicorn.acs.ttu.edu> via
  <http://www.ttu.edu/lists/acw-l> Accessed 1996
  Feb 17.

5 Newsgroup message

To document information posted in a **newsgroup** discussion, provide the following information:

- author's name (if known)
- author's email address, in angle brackets
- date of publication
- subject line from posting
- name of newsgroup, in angle brackets
- date of access

▶ ¹Slade R. <res@maths.bath.ac.uk>. 1996 Mar 26.
  UNIX made easy. <alt.books.reviews> Accessed
  1996 Mar 31.

If, after following all the suggestions in 4c-3, you cannot
determine the author's name, then use the author's email
address, enclosed in angle brackets, as the main entry.

▶ ²<lrm583@aol.com> 1996 May 26. Thinking of adoption. <alt.adoption> Accessed 1996 May 29.

6 Synchronous communication

To document a **synchronous communication**, such as those posted in **MOOs**, **MUDs**, and **IRCs**, provide the following information:

- name of speaker(s) (if known), or name of site
- date of event
- title of event (if appropriate)
- type of communication (group discussion, personal interview), if not indicated elsewhere in entry, in square brackets
- address, using a URL (in angle brackets) or command-line directions
- date of access

▶ [1]LambdaMOO. 1996 May 28. Seminar discussion on netiquette. <telnet://lambda.parc.xerox.edu :8888> Accessed 1996 May 28.

▶ [2]Harnack A. 1996 Apr 4. Words. [Group discussion]. telnet moo.du.org/port=8888 Accessed 1996 Apr 5.

7 Telnet site

To document a **telnet** site or a file available via telnet, provide the following information:

- author's name (if known)
- date of publication
- title of document (if known) (otherwise use *n.d.*)
- title of full work (if applicable)
- word *telnet*
- complete telnet address, with no closing punctuation
- directions for accessing document
- date of access

▶ [1]Aquatic Conservation Network. n.d. About the Aquatic Conservation Network. National Capital Freenet. telnet freenet.carleton.ca login as guest, go acn, press 1 Accessed 1996 May 28.

▶ [2]California Department of Pesticide Regulation. n.d. Pest management information. CSU Fresno

ATI-NET. telnet caticsuf.csufresno.edu login as
super, press a, press k Accessed 1996 May 28.

8 FTP site

To document a file available for downloading via **file
transfer protocol**, provide the following information:

- author's name (if known)
- date of publication (if known) (otherwise use *n.d.*)
- title of document
- abbreviation *ftp*
- address of FTP site, with no closing punctuation
- full path to follow to find document, with no closing
  punctuation
- date of access

▶ [1]Altar TW. 1993 Jan 14. Vitamin B12 and vegans.
ftp wiretap.spies.com Library/Article/Food
/b12.txt Accessed 1996 May 28.

You can use a URL (enclosed in angle brackets) instead of
the command, address, and path elements.

▶ [2]Matloff N. n.d. Immigration forum. <ftp://
heather.cs.ucdavis.edu/pub/Immigration/Index
.html> Accessed 1996 May 28.

9 Gopher site

To document information obtained by using the **gopher**
search protocol, provide the following information:

- author's name (if known)
- date of publication
- title of document
- any print publication information
- URL, in angle brackets
- date of access

▶ [1]Smith CA. 1994. National extension model of
critical parenting practices. <gopher://tinman
.mes.umn.edu:4242/11/Other/Other/NEM_Parent>
Accessed 1996 May 28.

To document the location of information using a gopher command-path format, give the following information instead of the URL:

- word *gopher*
- site name
- path followed to access document, with slashes to indicate menu selections

▶ [2]Commons sense: a viewer's guide to the British House of Commons. n.d. gopher c-span.org Transcripts and Publications/C-SPAN Publications/Commons Sense Accessed 1996 May 29.

10 Linkage data

To document a specific file and give **linkage data** showing its hypertext context, provide the following information:

- author's name (if known)
- date of publication (if known)
- title of document
- abbreviation *Lkd.* ("linked from")
- title of document to which file is linked
- additional linkage details (if applicable), preceded by *at*
- URL for source document, in angle brackets
- date of access

▶ [1]Hoemann GH. 1995 Nov 3. Electronic style-- elements of citation. Lkd. Electronic style page, at Continue and Citation elements. <http://funnelweb.utcc.utk.edu/~hoemann /style.html> Accessed 1996 May 29.

▶ [2]Miller A. n.d. Allison Miller's home page. Lkd. EKU honors program home page, at Personal pages. <http://www.csc.eku.edu/honors> Accessed 1996 Apr 2.

CHAPTER NINE

Using Images and Graphics

The Internet offers a rich treasury of images, icons, graphs, charts, maps, tables, reproductions of paintings, digital photographs, and many other visuals that you can easily **download** and use to illustrate your writing or part of a Web page. This chapter explains how to find images on the **World Wide Web** and use them in your work.

9a Finding images and graphics

With a graphic **browser**, you can visit museums such as the Louvre, view the paintings of Vincent Van Gogh and Marcel Duchamp, examine architectural plans in detail, investigate mechanical drawings, peruse weather maps, enjoy film clips of rock concerts, and inspect photographs taken by the Hubble Space Telescope. The following **Web sites**, among many others, provide extended lists of background patterns, wallpaper, images, and icons that anyone can download:

Arizona State's Graphics Warehouse
<http://www.eas.asu.edu/~graphics>

Provides background samplers, a color index, and numerous useful graphics such as arrows, balls, buttons, dingbats, and a variety of icons and lines.

The Background Sampler
<http://www.fciencias.unam.mx/ejemplo/index_bkgr.html>

Provides numerous background patterns useful for designing attractive Web pages.

The Icon Browser
<http://www.cli.di.unipi.it/iconbrowser/icons.html>

Gives access to 7,424 symbols and miscellaneous icons, plus a search engine.

Multimedia and Clip-art
<http://www.itec.sfsu.edu/multimedia/multimedia.html>

A site administered by the San Francisco State University's Department of Instructional Technologies that provides links to clip art, icons, graphics and "World Art Treasures."

Netscape: The Background Sampler
<http://www.netscape.com/assist/net_sites/bg/backgrounds.html>

Offers a wide range of backgrounds, from raindrops to stucco effects.

WebMuseum Network <http://watt.emf.net/wm/net>

Gives access to more than 10 million documents containing drawings and paintings from famous museum collections throughout the world.

Yahoo! Computers and Internet: Graphics
<http://www.yahoo.com/Computers_and_Internet/Graphics>

A useful Web page with links to clip art, computer animation, computer-generated graphics, exhibits, holography, morphing, and visualization software.

9b Using images and graphics

When you use images to support textual information, choose visuals that reinforce what you say in your text, so that the visuals help your readers understand your document. Andrea Lunsford and Robert Connors in *The St. Martin's Handbook* (New York: St. Martin's Press, 1997) offer the following tips for using visuals:

- *Use tables* to draw readers' attention to particular numerical information.

- *Use pie charts* to compare a part to the whole. Use *bar charts* and *line graphs* to compare one element with another, to compare elements over time, to demonstrate correlations, and to illustrate frequency.

- *Use drawings or diagrams* to draw attention to dimensions and to details.

- *Use maps* to draw attention to location and to spatial relationships.

- *Use cartoons* to illustrate or emphasize a point dramatically or to amuse.

- *Use photographs* to draw attention to a graphic scene (such as devastation following an earthquake) or to depict an object.

In short, base your choices on the purpose of your document and the needs of your audience.

9c Downloading images and graphics

When you use images and graphics in Web page designs, be selective. Because it may take many minutes to download a large graphic, good Web-text designers use illustrations only when these deliver information in a way that the text cannot. To help your readers use their browsers efficiently, choose graphics and images that can be transmitted quickly.

The two most common image file formats in use on the Web are **JPEG** (.jpeg or .jpg, pronounced "jay-peg") and **GIF** (.gif, pronounced "jiff" or "gif"). Although both formats can be used to include images in **hypertext** documents, they differ in several important ways. On the one hand, JPEG files are superior to GIF files for storing full-color or gray-scale images of "realistic" scenes such as scanned photographs. Any continuous variation in color will be represented more faithfully and in less disk space by JPEG files than by GIF files. On the other hand, GIF files work significantly better with images containing only a few distinct colors, such as line drawings and simple cartoons. As a rule, since low-resolution JPEG formats are suitable for computer display, use JPEG files whenever possible. For further information and advice, see "Frequently Asked Questions about JPEG Image Compression" at <http://www-inria-graphlib.inria.fr:8000/Faq/jpeg>.

To incorporate into your work graphics you find in other Web documents, first download the graphics to your computer and then create a link. Downloading images, graphics, backgrounds, and icons is generally easy. For example, if you're using the Netscape browser with a Windows 3.1 or Windows 95 operating system, you can download a copy of an image by using Netscape's pop-up menus. First, position your cursor over the image you want to download. Then click on the right mouse button. From the pop-up menu that now appears, choose "Save this image as," and type the appropriate information into the next **dialog box**. After you enter the information, the image will be downloaded to your computer.

If you're using a Macintosh, follow a similar procedure. Hold down the mouse button for about one second, choose "Save this image as" from the menu, and type the appropriate information into the box that appears. The image will now be quickly transmitted to your computer.

If your browser works with different commands, consult your Help menu.

9d Requesting permission to use images and graphics

Material that is copyrighted often includes a notice with the word *copyright*, the symbol ©, and the name of the copyright holder. This notice indicates that the material is protected by copyright and that unauthorized use is illegal. However, even material that doesn't include a notice is likely to be copyrighted. Assume material is copyrighted unless you know it is not.

EXAMPLE 9.1

```
MAIL TO:  malick@www.acm.uiuc.edu
CC TO:    stumiller@acs.eku.edu
SUBJECT:  Request for Permission
I am a student at Eastern Kentucky
University. I would like to request permis-
sion to download and use <escher-2worlds.gif>
as an illustration of M. C. Escher's work.
The illustration will be part of a class pro-
ject for my first-year composition course.
When using the image, I will cite
<http://www.acm.uiuc.edu:80/rml/Gifs/Escher>
as the URL, unless you specify a different
credit line. Thank you for considering my
request.
Alice Miller <stumiller@acs.eku.edu>
```

If you want to use a copyrighted graphic, icon, or image, then you need to write to the copyright holder and request permission to use the image. Example 9.1 shows a sample request for permission to use a digital reproduction of M. C. Escher's *Hands Drawing Hands*.

Depending on how you plan to use the image, the response to your request may indicate that a fee will be charged for use of the image. If the copyright holder denies permission, you can describe the graphic or image in words, refer your reader to the original URL, and perhaps explain your inability to use the graphic in a content note. Or you can look for another graphic suitable for your use.

For further information about requesting permissions to use Internet sources, see 10e.

9e Integrating images and graphics with text

When you use images in a paper or on a Web page, integrate all graphics into your text so that the images and text reinforce each other.

To help coordinate images and text on a Web page, many designers offer the following suggestions:

- Make readability a priority.
- Select background patterns that complement the subject matter of the Web page. For example, many Web-page designers use muted and textured backgrounds that effectively foreground dark-colored textual information.
- Choose contrasting colors for text and background.
- Remember that busy backgrounds are distracting even when contrast is not a problem.
- Use images that are your own, that you have been given permission to use, or that are provided for anyone's use without charge.

Memory Made Manifest: The United States Holocaust Memorial Museum

By Laura Dove

There is a link which connects the collective memory of the American people with the horror of the Holocaust. When rain soaks the ground at the sites of Auschwitz, Dachau, and other death camps, shards of bone and layers of ash work their way to the surface. This same process is at work in our recollections of the Holocaust. Americans have been unable to suppress the guilt and horror that remembering the Holocaust engenders, and have slowly come to realize that events that occurred fifty years ago and thousands of miles away demand accomodation in our national conciousness. The United States Holocaust Memorial Museum is a facet of offical American memory fitted into the iconography of the Mall in Washington D.C. This project explores the nature of the Holocaust in the American consciousness culminating in the creation of the Holocaust Commission in 1978, the formation and development of the President's Commission on the Holocaust and the U.S. Holocaust Memorial Council, and the physical and emotional parameters of the exhibit it houses.

Contents

Figure 9.1
A Web document incorporating photography
This document has links to several related documents, one of which is shown in Figure 9.2. Laura Dove, Memory Made Manifest: The United States Holocaust Memorial Museum, n.d. <http://xroads.virginia.edu /~cap/holo/holo.html> (7 Nov. 1996).

- Keep your images as small as possible. Use a software program such as Paint Shop Pro or Photoshop to reduce the size of your image. Small files load faster and help ensure compatibility with all systems.

- In your Web document, link a thumbnail version of an image to the larger file. Your reader may then decide whether to download the larger image.

- Describe images in your **HTML** text for readers whose browsers don't accept graphics. Do this because users of text-only browsers see only the code [ISMAP], indicating that an image is not available.

The Architecture of the Holocaust Memorial

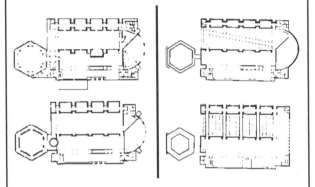

When architect James Ingo Freed accepted the commission to plan the United States Holocaust Memorial, he was nervous about the challenge of creating a building that expressed the enormity of the event. He recalled his reaction in a series of interviews with *Assemblage* magazine, saying "I have to make a building that allows for horror, sadness. I don't know if you can make a building that does this, if you can make an architecture of sensibility." In his plans for the United States Holocaust Memorial, Freed created a building of exceptional sensibility and impact. With a combination of evocative architectural language, sensitivity to the demands of his "clients" (the people of the United States, the members of the U.S. Commission on the Holocaust, and extensive government bureaucracy), and a creative approach to the requirements of the site and subject matter, Freed's building is (in the words of architectural critic Jim Murphy) "the most emotionally powerful architectural event most of us will ever experience." Freed's building utilizes the threads of American memory that undergird our conception of the Holocaust and represents an exceptionally successful architectural achievement.

With the final selection of James Freed as the architect for the memorial, the Holocaust began in earnest its quest to lend physical dimension to the horror of the Holocaust. After rejecting its initial plan to adapt existing buildings on the site, adjacent to the Mall, the commission envisaged a memorial tailored to the needs of the project and suited to the site. The building required space for a permanent exhibit, room for educational and research facilities, a place for peaceful contemplation (termed the Hall of Remembrance), and space for temporary exhibits. On October 16, 1985, the soil of the Mall was ritualistically mixed with soil from the concentration camps at the official groundbreaking. Elie Wiesel mused that, at the time, "we begin to lend a physical dimension to our relentless quest for remembrance" (Linenthal 57). For the next eight years, the planners and architects entrusted with making this memory manifest would struggle with the duty of creating a physical structure that was inclusive, unique, and evocative.

Figure 9.2
A Web document incorporating an architectural floor plan
Laura Dove, "The Architecture of the Holocaust Memorial," lkd. Memory Made Manifest: The United States Holocaust Memorial Museum, *n.d.<http://xroads.virginia.edu/~cap/holo/arch.html> (7 Nov. 1996).*

For information on how to insert a description of an image for such readers into an HTML document, see "The Lynx Manifesto" (5 Jan. 1996) at <http://world.std.com/~adamg/manifesto.html>.

- Place the copyright symbol © at the bottom of your page to remind your readers that your material may not be reproduced without your permission.

By following these suggestions for using graphics, you will not only complement and reinforce the content of your Web page but also present your readers with screens that are quickly loaded, easily read, and efficiently reproduced.

Using the guidelines in this chapter, a student produced the well-designed and informative Web documents shown in Figures 9.1 and 9.2.

To find more information about designing Web pages that incorporate images, visit the following sites:

Web Page Design
<http://www.uaa.alaska.edu/cas/jpc/webdesign.html>

David Siegel, *Web Wonk*
<http://www.dsiegel.com>

HTML/WWW Style Guides
<http://www.khoros.unm.edu/staff/neilb/weblint/style.html>

CHAPTER TEN

Publishing Texts on the Internet

From personal **email** to **newsgroup** postings, from **listserv** messages to **hypertext** essays on the **World Wide Web**, writing on the **Internet** brings many new opportunities to meet others, share ideas, and influence opinion. For writers entering the twenty-first century, taking advantage of such opportunities is now part and parcel of a writing education. Seek opportunities to write **online**—and have fun doing it! This chapter will help you enter the world of Internet publication.

10a Writing on the Internet

Colleges and universities now offer Internet courses in many disciplines. Some instructors in such courses teach paperless classes, requiring that all communication between them and students (and among students) be electronic. Others may require some submissions in print and some in electronic form.

Instructors committed to teaching courses electronically or promoting electronic communication in the classroom generally ask students to use email and often publish syllawebs (syllabi published on the Web) containing course information; they may also expect students to produce **webfolios** (collections of writings published on the Web). Listservs and **HyperNews** are two other electronic formats being required or recommended in many classes. Writing on the Internet brings new challenges, but it is not difficult and can be enormously satisfying.

10b Composing Web texts

You may have occasion to compose **hypertexts** for publication on the Web. A hypertext is a collection of documents containing links that let readers move easily from one document to another. Hypertexts may include graphics, sound, and video, in which case they are often referred to as hypermedia.

Hypertexts are created by formatting documents in **HTML**, a code for tagging **ASCII** texts, typefaces, type sizes, colors, graphics, and video to create **hyperlinks**. Using HTML is not difficult; you can learn to code with HTML in a few hours. Here is a section of a student's Web document with HTML codes visible, followed by the text with the codes hidden. Figure 10.1 shows part of the document as it appears when viewed with a graphic browser.

▶ ```
<html><head><title>The Mizzou MOO page</title>
</head>
<body bgcolor="#ffffff" vlink="#005500" link=
"#0000ff">
<img height=125 width=137 align=left src="moocow
.gif">
<h2>The Mizzou MOO page</h2>
<p>MOOs (MUD Object Oriented
or, to some, <i>Multiuser Object Oriented</i>
systems) are text-based virtual realities housed
on computers connected to the Internet. The
first of these was developed at the famous
```
```

```
<ahref="http://www.parc.xerox.com/"><b>Xerox
PARC</b> (<i>Palo Alto Research Center</i>)</a>
by Pavel Curtis (aka Haakon, aka Lambda) and is
known as <ahref="telnet://lambda.parc.xerox
.com:8888/"><b>LambdaMOO</b></a>. </p>
```

The Mizzou MOO page

MOOs (*MUD Object Oriented* or, to some, *Multiuser Object Oriented* systems) are text-based virtual realities housed on computers connected to the Internet. The first of these was developed at the famous **Xerox PARC** *(Palo Alto Research Center)* by Pavel Curtis (aka Haakon, aka Lambda) and is known as **LambdaMOO**.

You can find guides to composing hypertext documents both in bookstores and on the Web (by searching for HTML writing guides). Here are some of the most popular and useful guides available on the Web:

A Beginner's Guide to HTML
<http://www.ncsa.uiuc.edu/General/Internet/WWW/HTMLPrimer.html>

An introduction to using HTML and creating files for the Web, with links to additional information.

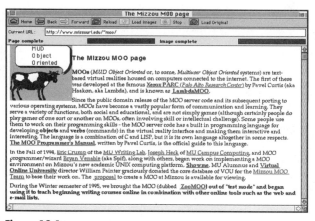

Figure 10.1
An HTML document viewed with a graphic browser
"The Mizzou MOO Page," 12 Aug. 1996 <http://www.missouri.edu/~moo> (8 Nov. 1996).

HTML Quick Reference (Michael Grobe)
<http://www.cc.ukans.edu/info/HTML_quick.html>

A concise reference guide that lists the most commonly used elements from Versions 1 and 2 of HTML and briefly describes each element.

HTML Reference Manual *(Sandia National Laboratories)*
<http://www.sandia.gov/sci_compute/html_ref.html>

Provides a comprehensive list of HTML elements.

Composing Good HTML
<http://www.cs.cmu.edu/~tilt/cgh>

Version 2.0.4 addresses stylistic points of HTML composition at both the document and the Web level.

For a longer list of guides, see *Guides to Writing Style for HTML Documents* at <http://union.ncsa.uiuc.edu/Hyper News/get/www/html/guides.html>. Continually updated to include new coding, HTML guides are useful for beginning as well as more advanced HTML writers.

Numerous software programs for creating HTML texts (known as HTML editors) are also available. For descriptions and evaluations, consult one or more of the following:

> *World Wide Web and HTML Tools*
> <http://www.w3.org/pub/WWW/Tools>

> *Publishing on the Web*
> <http://pix.za/pix/publish.html>

> *HTML Editors: The Consummate Winsock Apps List*
> <http://caboose.com/CWSApps/html.html>

When writing for the Web, follow these general principles:

Guidelines for composing Web pages
- If necessary, make sure all documents are approved for publication by your institution.
- Give each page a title.
- Make the text of your document easy to scan. To spare your readers the tedium of moving a cursor up and down a long text, keep the text relatively short.

- Organize your document so that supporting material can be accessed through links. Long definitions and explanations, digressions, illustrations, statistics, notes, bibliographies, and forms to be completed—all these can be in separate documents linked to the main document.

- Create internal links that let readers go quickly from one part of the document to another (e.g., from a sub-section to the table of contents).

- Keep the information within a document current.

- Make sure that each page in a collection has a link to the collection's homepage.

- Provide text transcripts for audio clips.

10c Designing homepages

Your **homepage** is the HTML document in which you welcome readers to your Web site and steer them to the links and documents available at the site. Personal home-pages typically include biographies, graphics, photographs, lists of links, tables, dates of construction and revisions, and the author's email address(es). Business homepages may carry logos, product announcements and reviews, links to corporate representatives, and forms for making online transactions.

If you're affiliated with a college or university, find out whether it enables students to place homepages on the Web. Visit your institution's homepage to acquaint yourself with its policies regarding student Web publications. The homepage may also offer style recommendations and online help as well as links to research sites and to outside sites providing information on coding HTML texts. For a list of policies and guidelines for designing university-approved Web pages, visit *WWW Policies AND Guidelines* at <http://www.lib.muohio.edu/~skimmel/wwwpols.html>.

An excellent way to get ideas for your own homepage is to explore the work of other Web authors. For a look at especially innovative homepage designs, visit one or more of these Web sites:

Cool Site of the Day
<http://cool.infi.net>
Presents one attractively designed new site each day.

Personal Pages World Wide
<http://www.utexas.edu/world/personal/index.html>
Contains links to collections of personal pages at universities worldwide.

To design effective, readable homepages, follow these guidelines:

Designing effective homepages
- Use horizontal rules to separate sections.
- Use text highlighting (e.g., italic and bold type) sparingly.
- Use a footer at the bottom of the page for general information (e.g., the site's URL, a *mailto* connection to the page's owner, the owner's email address, the date of last modification) and separate the footer from the body of the text with a horizontal rule.
- Use your institution's or agency's logo where appropriate.
- Use thumbnail images as links to larger images.
- Describe images in your text for readers using text-only browsers. (See 9e.)
- Give the date when the document was last updated.
- If the homepage is moved to a new site, leave a notice at the old location directing readers to the new site.

See Figure 10.2 for an example of an inviting homepage.

Many Web page designers offer advice and provide examples of their work. You may find especially helpful David Siegel's *Web Wonk* at <http://www.dsiegel.com> and Patrick J. Lynch's *Web Style Manual* at <http://info.med.yale.edu/caim/StyleManual_Top.HTML>.

10d Avoiding plagiarism and acknowledging sources

Plagiarism, defined as the fraudulent presentation of someone else's work as your own, is almost universally condemned. Nearly all style manuals explain why plagiarism must be avoided and how to give credit to other writers when citing their ideas or wording. Moreover, most colleges and universities have official policies concerning plagiarism and specific penalties for punishing

Welcome to the **Meldrum Family Genealogy** page. Here you will find information about my MELDRUM family and related families; soon I will also post information about other MELDRUM lines I know of. For information beyond what is on this page, please contact me.

The Families

My **MELDRUM** line comes from Scotland through Nova Scotia to Maine. James C. MELDRUM settled in Lunenburg, Nova Scotia, around 1783. Most of the MELDRUMs stayed there until early in the twentieth century, when some moved into New Brunswick and Maine.

The MELDRUM Family
My All-Names List
My Related Families
My Tiny Tafel

Other Resources

These resources relate somehow to the **MELDRUM** Family, my related families, or genealogy in general.

The Genealogical Association of Nova Scotia
Parker Barrington's page, with Nova Scotia genealogy info.
New Brunswick Genealogy
The Genealogy Home Page
Meldrum House, Oldmeldrum, Scotland.
Meldrum Bay, Ontario, named for the Michigan MELDRUM family.

page maintained by Ron Meldrum, rmeldrum@bates.edu
photos: upper left: James Sporden Meldrum, Adelia [Wagner] Meldrum (holding Earnest Meldrum), and Wallace Meldrum, c. 1922; **lower right**: Ada [Bishop] Henry and Herman Henry, c. 1930.

This page is dedicated in memory of **Lora Mildred [HENRY] Meldrum** (1902-1993), the best grandmother a grandson could want.

`7 5 3`
reset 1/1/96

Counter indicates number of hits   **Rules separate sections**

Footer gives information about page

Figure 10.2
The *Meldrum Family Genealogy* homepage
This Web page integrates photos, graphics, and text into a succinct, appealing, and informative document. The hotlinks in its tables of contents allow readers to delve further into the Meldrum family's background or to explore sites related to the broader topic of genealogy. Ron Meldrum, Meldrum Family Genealogy, 10 Oct. 1996 <http://www.bates.edu /~rmeldrum> (22 Oct. 1996).

offenders. (See, for example, the *Carnegie Mellon University Policy on Cheating and Plagiarism* at <http://infoserver.andrew.cmu.edu/policy/documents/Cheating.html>.)

The Internet makes it easy for you to use other sources in your writing and encourages collaboration among its users. As a result, the traditional notion of the "author" as a single individual working alone on his or her document can be difficult to maintain in an online context. Many software programs promote group writing in the form of collaborative drafting, editing, and revision. Such "patch-writing" means that our print-based notions about who "owns" a text—and what exactly constitutes an *author*—must now be rethought and perhaps redefined.[1]

The fourth edition of the *MLA Handbook for Writers of Research Papers* by Joseph Gibaldi (Modern Language Association, 1995) recognizes that certain forms of writing often involve collaborative efforts, which the traditional guidelines regarding plagiarism do not always address:

> [One] issue concerns collaborative work, such as a group project you carry out with other students. Joint participation in research and writing is common and, in fact, encouraged in many courses and in many professions, and it does not constitute plagiarism provided that credit is given for all contributions. One way to give credit, if roles were clearly demarcated or were unequal, is to state exactly who did what. Another way, especially if roles and contributions were merged and truly shared, is to acknowledge all concerned equally. Ask your instructor for advice if you are not certain how to acknowledge collaboration. (29)

Authors of print sources commonly acknowledge participants in collaborative writing projects at the beginning of a book, essay, or research report, often in a preface or note. Internet writers, too, must acknowledge help from other authors and researchers, as well as from page designers, graphic artists, funding institutions, and software developers. In your hypertext document, you can dedicate a separate linked page to acknowledging help and sources. Example 10.1 shows an extract from a typical acknowledgments page.

---

[1] See, for example, Rebecca Howard, *Standing in the Shadow of Giants: Plagiarism and Writer-Text Collaboration in Composition Pedagogy* (Norwood, NJ: Ablex, forthcoming).

EXAMPLE 10.1

Acknowledgments

Project Censored Canada (PCC) is very much a collective effort. We wish to thank the journalists who wrote the underreported stories; the magazines and newspapers that published them; and the journalists, activists, and other interested individuals who nominated the stories. We also wish to thank the researchers, students participating in PCC seminars at both Simon Fraser University and the University of Windsor in the spring of 1995. Our researchers analyzed approximately 150 nominations to determine if they qualified as underreported stories and then selected the top eighteen for forwarding to our distinguished national panel of judges, to whom thanks are also due.

Student Researchers

Diane Burgess, Laurie Dawkins, Cameron Dempsey, Chantal Ducoeurjoly, Bill Duvall, James Duvall, Shoni Field, David Fittler, Rita Fromholt, Tony Fusaro, Dale Gamble, Madelaine Halls, Clayton Jones, Ava Lew, Cheryl Linstead, Kirsten Madsen, Lauren Maris, Jennifer Morrison, Carmen Pon, Elizabeth Rains, Steve Rennie, Humaira Shah, Karen Whale, and Tracy Workman.

"Project Censored Canada: Researching the Nation's News Agenda. A joint project of the School of Communication, Simon Fraser University Department of Communication Studies, University of Windsor." 25 Apr. 1996. <http://cc6140mac.comm.sfu.ca/acknowledgements.html> (26 June 1996).

When you engage in online composition and publication, not only do you open yourself to the possibilities of collaboration, you also assume responsibility for acknowledging the influences that make such writing possible.

10e Requesting permission to use copyrighted sources

You are free to access and read any material that is published on the Internet. Whenever you reproduce information found on the Internet, however, you are in fact disseminating that information and thus may need to seek permission to use it. Material that is copyrighted often includes a notice with the word *copyright*, the symbol ©, and the name of the copyright holder (e.g., "This paper's contents on paper and in any electronic form are copyrighted © 1995 by Anita F. Colyer. All rights reserved."). Such a notice indicates that the material is protected by copyright and that unauthorized use is illegal. However, even material that doesn't include a notice is likely to be copyrighted. Asssume material is copyrighted unless you know it is not.

If you want to use part or all of a copyrighted document, then you need to write to the copyright holder and request permission to use the desired text, image, or file. Example 10.2 is a request for permission to reproduce a copyrighted text.

If permission is granted, then you may use the source as you have indicated. If permission is denied, however, you must respect the denial. You may, of course, create a hyperlink to the source itself, refer to the source, or paraphrase or summarize its contents, citing the source appropriately. If necessary, include in your paper a content note explaining your use of a particular source.

In an educational, noncommercial setting, "fair use" of copyrighted materials is allowed. Fair use provisions in copyright law usually designate some copying as legal. The intent is to increase public access to the work without infringing on the benefits derived from the work by the author or publisher. Generally, fair use of copyrighted material for personal, noncommercial use is not a copyright infringement.

Laws regarding rights to intellectual property available on the Internet continue to evolve. If you need answers to questions about copyright law, permissions, and good ethical practice, turn to the Internet for up-to-date information on these subjects. The sites listed in Box 10.1 provide useful information.

10f Citing Internet sources in hypertext essays

A hypertext essay often contains links to sources cited in the text. For this reason, some instructors do not require their students to append a list of works cited when they are citing only Internet sources in an essay. If all of the

EXAMPLE 10.2

```
MAIL TO:  IN%"afc@cde.psu.edu"
CC TO:    stumiller@acs.eku.edu
SUBJECT:  Request for permission
Anita F. Colyer,
I wish to request permission to quote from
Part I of your "Copyright Law and the
Internet." Quotations from your text will
appear in a research paper to be submitted
in my webfolio (collection of online
writings). The paper will, in part, help
writers do research on the Internet. I
will, of course, give credit to you as the
author of my source and will specify
<http://Clair.ce.psu.edu/de/ide/Colyer.html>
as the original URL. Please let me know if
such permission is granted. Thank you.
Alice Miller <stumiller@acs.eku.edu>
```

sources are already connected to the HTML text, readers can retrieve them without a separate list.

Since Internet sites can easily be revised, archived, or even removed from the Internet, some instructors require a list of sources even for a hypertext essay citing only Internet sources. Such a list provides a handy summary of all the Internet sources used in the essay and demonstrates the nature and extent of the author's research. Also, readers may need to know not only the date of a posting but also the date when the writer accessed the site. Such information, while not available from linkage data contained in essays formatted in HTML, can be made available in a list of sources cited. This information

---

Box 10.1
Sites providing information on copyright issues

The Copyright Act of 1976
<http://www.law.cornell.edu/uscode/17>

Cyberspace Law for Non-Lawyers
<http://www.counsel.com/cyberspace>

Intellectual Property
<http://www.benton.org/KickStart/kick.intellectualproperty.html>

Copyright Law and the Internet (Anita F. Colyer)
<http://Clair.ce.psu.edu/de/ide/Colyer.html>

can help readers determine the currency and reliability of the Internet information. For these reasons—in order to enable readers to review the scope of a writer's research and determine posting and access dates—many instructors require a list of works cited even in hypertext essays. If you are required to provide a list of Internet works cited, see Chapters 5–8 for guidelines for citing and documenting Internet sources. You are never wrong to include a list of works cited; if you're not sure of your instructor's requirements, provide such a list.

10g Obtaining a URL for your publication

To enable readers to find your homepage using common Internet **search tools**, you must register it. Since no one registration automatically places your work on the entire World Wide Web, choose a registration service that suits your needs and appeals to your intended audiences. Some but not all registration sites charge for this service. To examine sites where you can register your homepage and other publications, visit *Web Referencing Kit* at <http://apollo.co.uk/web-kit.html>.

To speed up the registration process, have the following information ready:

• Your document's title
• A brief description of your document
• An accurate transcription of your URL (*http* address)
• A list of keywords that people searching for your site are likely to use
• A list of categories your site would fit into in an index of topics

You are now ready to register your publication with one or more search tools.

Once you have registered your homepage, people are likely not only to read your publication but also to correspond with you about it. Reply promptly to any correspondence you receive.

10h Observing netiquette

As a writer on the Internet, observe online conventions of behavior so that you can communicate effectively.

Netiquette (the etiquette of the Internet) refers to the rhetorical courtesies writers use when communicating with others online. Arlene Rinaldi's "The Net: User Guidelines and Netiquette" at <http://www.vir.com /neti/index.html> provides valuable guidance for communicating via email, **telnet**, **FTP**, newsgroups, the Web, and so on. Here, for example, is Rinaldi's advice about using email, listservs, and newsgroups:

Arlene Rinaldi's netiquette guidelines

- Keep paragraphs and messages short and to the point.

- Focus on one subject per message and always include a pertinent subject title for the message so that the user can locate the message quickly.

- Don't use the academic networks for commercial work.

- Include your "signature" at the bottom of email messages by providing a footer that includes your name, position, affiliation, and Internet . . . address. The footer should not exceed four lines. If you wish, you can also provide your address and phone number.

- Capitalize words only to highlight an important point or to distinguish a title or heading.

- Use *asterisks* before and after a word to make a stronger point. Avoid capitalizing whole words that are not titles, a practice that is generally termed SHOUTING!

- Limit line length.

- Follow chain-of-command procedures for corresponding with superiors. For example, don't send a complaint via email directly to the top just because you can.

- Be professional and careful in what you say about others. Email is easily forwarded.

- Cite all quotations, references, and sources and respect copyright and license agreements.

- It is considered extremely rude to forward personal email to mailing lists or Usenet without the original author's permission.

- Be careful when using sarcasm and humor. Without the benefit of face-to-face communication, your joke may be viewed as criticism.

- Acronyms (e.g., IMHO, in my humble/honest opinion) can be used to abbreviate when possible; however, messages that are filled with acronyms can confuse and annoy the reader.

Many groups and associations that maintain listservs and newsgroups describe their norms of online conduct in **FAQ** ("fack," or frequently asked question) documents. FAQs provide answers to questions that people new to a given group are likely to ask. The following excerpt is from a FAQ posted by Philippe Brieu, Walter I. Nissen Jr., and Steven Willner in <sci.astro>, a newsgroup devoted to the discussion of all aspects of astronomy.

> What are the guidelines for posting on astro newsgroups?
> If you will follow this group for a month or so before posting here, you will greatly reduce the likelihood that you will participate in making the newsgroup less productive and friendly and then end up regretting it. If you are new here, it is likely that any question you want to ask has already been asked. If so, its answer is probably in one of the FAQ files. Check out the newsgroups news.answers, sci.answers, and news .announce.newusers, or ask your local help file or administrator to point you toward the FAQs. . . . Certain topics repeatedly come up and lead to lengthy, loud-mouthed discussions that never lead anywhere interesting. Often these topics have extremely little to do with the science of astronomy. . . . It would also help if you would ask yourself a few simple questions before posting:
> Is this post about the science of astronomy?
> Will many of the thousands and thousands of readers here, people interested in the science of astronomy, find it of personal benefit?
> If you do ask a question, please consider writing up the answer for a FAQ file. . . .

This FAQ and many others like it also cover issues such as posting test messages, posting inordinately long messages, and spamming (sending unsolicited advertisements).

When you communicate in cyberspace, remember that your readers represent a multitude of cultures, interests, and viewpoints. As an Internet writer, respect the expectations and needs of the particular audience you happen to be addressing.

A Directory of Internet Sources

This appendix lists URLs that make good starting points for doing research in most academic disciplines and areas of professional specialization. Each section (e.g., Earth sciences) includes two groups of URLs: the first group gives one or more Web addresses listing current hotlinks in a given area, and the second group lists sample Web postings and publications in a given field.

Because the number of Web sites grows daily, no printed list of URLs is entirely up-to-date. In addition to using this directory, remember to visit the *Online!* Web site at <http://www.smpcollege.com/online-4styles~help>, where the directory is archived and continually updated. Bookmark this Web site so that you can easily visit it.

Sources for the following list include the Argus Clearinghouse at <http://www.clearinghouse.net>, the WWW Virtual Library at <http://www.w3.org/vl/Overview.html>, and the "Information Technology Resources" pages in the *Chronicle of Higher Education*, which are compiled by Bianca P. Floyd.

a Accounting

Rutgers Accounting Web
<http://www.rutgers.edu/Accounting/raw.html> is "an accounting information retrieval system, available on the Internet for use by accounting scholars, practitioners, educators, and students."

Sample sites

Financial Executives Institute
<http://www.fei.org> seeks to help chief financial officers, vice presidents of finance, treasurers, and controllers enhance their professional skills and their companies' operations.

Maxwell Technologies Taxing Times

<http://www.scubed.com/tax/tax.html> tracks changing tax regulations.

b   Archaeology

Archaeology on the World Wide Web

<http://www.swan.ac.uk/classics/antiquity.html> discusses the impact of the Web on archaeology.

ArchNet

<http://spirit.lib.uconn.edu/archnet> gives links to news, museums, and academic departments.

Sample site

Pompeii Forum Project

<http://jefferson.village.virginia.edu/pompeii/page-1.html> is a photographic and textual research report.

c   Arts (performing and fine arts)

Visual & Performing Arts INFOMINE

<http://lib-www.ucr.edu/vpainfo.html> is a comprehensive index to Web resources.

WWW Virtual Library: Music

<http://syy.oulu.fi/music> categorizes links by instrument, performer, composer, genre, and so on.

Sample sites

ArtsEdge

<http://artsedge.kennedy-center.org> is "linking the arts and education through technology."

ArtsNet

<http://artsnet.heinz.cmu.edu> includes a Career Resources Center and a listing of cultural resources.

The Fine Arts Museums of San Francisco
<http://www.thinker.org> are making their entire collection of 60,000 works of art available online.

d Astronomy

The Astronomy Cafe
<http://www2.ari.net/home/odenwald/cafe.html> provides an introduction to astronomy and astronomical research.

WWW-VL: Astronomy and Astrophysics & AstroWeb
<http://www.w3.org/vl/astro/astro.html> links the major databases for astronomical research.

Sample site

The Observatorium
<http://observe.ivv.nasa.gov> offers "pictures of the earth, planets, stars, and other cool stuff, as well as the stories behind those images" from the National Aeronautics and Space Administration.

e Biology

The WWW Virtual Library: Biosciences
<http://golgi.harvard.edu/biopages> categorizes biology resources by type of provider and by subject.

Sample sites

The Biology Place
<http://www.biology.com> lists resources for introductory biology courses and invites users to post questions to experts.

Hawaii Biological Server
<http://www.bishop.hawaii.org/bishop/HBS/hbs1
.html> includes sections on botany, entomology, and ichthyology.

f Business and economics

Internet Business Library

<http://www.bschool.ukans.edu/intbuslib/virtual.htm>
has links to news, data, and research reports on domestic and international business and trade.

Madalyn, a Business Research Tool

<http://www.udel.edu/alex/mba/main/netdir2.html>
focuses on all aspects of business administration.

Sample sites

Better Business Bureau

<http://www.bbb.org/bbb> provides a directory of
offices and services, product information, and links to
other consumer and business resources.

MCB University Press

<http://www.mcb.co.uk> offers management news
and information, including links to disaster prevention
journals.

g Chemistry

ChemCenter

<http://www.chemcenter.org> is a service of the
American Chemical Society.

The WWW Virtual Library: Chemistry

<http://www.chem.ucla.edu/chempointers.html> provides links to Web, gopher, and FTP sites and Usenet
newsgroups for all aspects of chemistry.

Sample sites

Molecule of the Month and Molecules of the Month

<http://www.bris.ac.uk/Depts/Chemistry/MOTM
/motm.htm> and <http://www.ch.ic.ac.uk/motm>
provide graphic reports on an ever-increasing list of
molecules.

Moviemol

<http://chem-www.mps.ohio-state.edu/~lars/movie mol.html> demonstrates software that creates three-dimensional images of molecules from any angle or distance.

h Classics

Classics and Mediterranean Archaeology Home Page

<http://rome.classics.lsa.umich.edu/welcome.html> collects sources on topics ranging from ABZU to Xanten.

Sample sites

Diotima: Materials for the Study of Women and Gender in the Ancient World

<http://www.uky.edu/ArtsSciences/Classics/gender .html> holds course descriptions, essays, and images.

The Perseus Project

<http://www.perseus.tufts.edu> is "an evolving digital library on ancient Greece and Rome."

i Communications

Media Web Guide

<http://www.mcs.net/~kfliegel/media/media.html> links resources for newspapers, magazines, television, radio, and online media.

Sample sites

The First Amendment Handbook

<http://www.rcfp.org/1stamend> is a service of the Reporters Committee for Freedom of the Press.

Project Censored

<http://zippy.sonoma.edu/ProjectCensored> explores the extent of censorship in the United States.

j Computer science

The WWW Virtual Library: Computing

<http://src.doc.ic.ac.uk/bySubject/Computing/Over
view.html> offers links to an online dictionary of computing and to the Internet Computer Index, as well as to thousands of bibliographies and technical reports.

Sample sites

Association of Shareware Professionals

<http://www.asp-shareware.org> includes news of the latest software produced by ASP members.

The Year 2000 Information Center

<http://www.year2000.com> reviews the host of problems anticipated in 2000 for computer systems and software that handle year numbers with only two digits.

k Earth sciences

Consortium for International Earth Science Information Network

<http://www.gateway.ciesin.org> "facilitates access to data and information on human interactions in the environment, global environmental changes, and sustainable development."

Websurfer's Weekly Earth Sciences Review: Hotlinks Section

<http://rainbow.rmii.com/~michaelg/HOTLINKS
.html> compiles Web and listserv information for geography, geology, hydrology, paleontology, and related subjects.

Sample sites

Great Globe Gallery

<http://hum.amu.edu.pl/~zbzw/glob/glob1.htm> offers more than sixty views of the earth.

Monterey Bay Aquarium Research Institute

<http://www.mbari.org> provides access to oceano-graphic Web resources, with data updated every ten minutes.

Education

The WWW Virtual Library: Education

<http://www.csu.edu.au/education/library.html> cate-gorizes information sources by subject and permits online searching.

Sample sites

From Now On: The Educational Technology Journal

<http://www.pacificrim.net/~mckenzie> promotes "strategies to engage students in problem-solving, invention, and discovery."

Model Education Systems Association

<http://www.sunspace.com/main.htm> provides demographic data on U.S. public school systems and information on technology in schools.

English

The English Server at Carnegie-Mellon University

<http://english-www.hss.cmu.edu> offers links to resources for more than 10,000 texts in many disciplines.

Sample sites

Early Modern Literary Studies

<http://purl.oclc.org/emls/emlshome.html> is an elec-tronic journal for research into 16th- and 17th-century English literature.

The Purdue University On-Line Writing Lab and the **Virginia Tech Online Writing Lab**

<http://owl.english.purdue.edu> and <http://athena .english.vt.edu/OWL_WWW/OWL.html> feature

online writing tutors and links to files to help with
grammar and style

n   Environmental studies

The WWW Virtual Library: Environment

<http://ecosys.drdr.virginia.edu/Environment.html>
includes links to resources in biodiversity, environmental law, forestry, and landscape architecture.

Sample sites

COOL: Conservation On-Line

<http://palimpsest.stanford.edu> is "a full-text database
of conservation information."

The Nature Conservancy

<http://www.tnc.org> offers "the opportunity to learn
about and help protect endangered animals, plants, and
habitats at the click of a button."

o   Ethnic studies

Black/African Related Resources

<http://www.sas.upenn.edu/African_Studies/Home
_Page/mcgee.html> lists information sites concerning
Black or African people, culture, and issues around the
world.

The WWW Virtual Library: Migration and Ethnic
Relations

<http://www.ruu.nl/ercomer/wwwvl> is a collection of
links to major Internet resources provided by the
European Documentation Centre and Observatory on
Migration and Ethnic Relations.

Sample sites

NativeWeb

<http://web.maxwell.syr.edu/nativeweb> provides a
"cyber-place for Earth's indigenous peoples."

W. E. B. DuBois Institute for Afro-American Research

<http://web-dubois.fas.harvard.edu/DuBois.html> provides information about the history, culture, and social institutions of African Americans.

p   Gender studies

Feminist Internet Gateway

<http://www.feminist.org/gateway/1_gatway.html> lists resources on topics such as women's health, women in politics, women and work, feminist arts, and violence against women.

infoQueer: The Queer Infoservers List

<http://www.infoqueer.org/queer/qis> provides the Queer Infoservers List, a collection of resources on gay and lesbian topics.

Men's Issues Page

<http://www.vix.com/men> aims "to cover the several men's movements encyclopedically."

Sample sites

American Fathers Coalition

<http://www.erols.com/afc> aims "to promote positive father-inclusive policies on a federal legislative and regulatory level."

Feminist Majority Foundation

<http://www.feminist.org> offers information on feminist issues and concerns.

q   Health and medicine

HealthFAQ

<http://www.healthfaq.com> is "designed for those who want to lead healthier lives and those who want to

take an active role in dealing with illness, injury, and disability."

MedNet Links

<http://www.mednet-i.com/links.html> is a service of COR Healthcare Resources.

Sample sites

ACSM Online

<http://www.a1.com/sportsmed> provides information from the American College of Sports Medicine.

Chronic IllNet

<http://www.calypte.com> offers links to news and research reports about chronic illnesses, including AIDS.

r History

Horus' History Links

<http://www.ucr.edu/h-gig/horuslinks.html> is maintained by the Department of History at University of California–Riverside.

Internet Resources in History

<http://www.tntech.edu/www/acad/hist/resources .html> is maintained by the Department of History at Tennessee Technological University.

Sample sites

CROMOHS

<http://www.unifi.it/riviste/cromohs/> is the *CyberReview of Modern Historiography.*

Siege and Commune of Paris

<http://www.library.nwu.edu:80/spec/siege>, from Northwestern University Library's Special Collections, contains links to more than 1,200 photographs taken in 1870 and 1871.

s   Humanities

Voice of the Shuttle

<http://humanitas.ucsb.edu> weaves together academic, professional, and scholarly resources for humanities research.

Webliography: A Guide to Internet Resources

<http://www.lib.lsu.edu/weblio.html#Humanities> includes links for all the humanities including architecture, art, classics, film, history, literature, music, philosophy, and theater.

Sample sites

Humanist Discussion Group

<http://www.princeton.edu/~mccarty/humanist> focuses on the application of computers to the humanities.

CH Working Papers

<http://www.chass.utoronto.ca:8080/epc/chwp> from the University of Toronto and King's College (London) is "an interdisciplinary series of refereed publications on computer-assisted research."

t   International studies

The WWW Virtual Library: International Affairs Resources

<http://www.pitt.edu/~ian/ianres.html> categorizes information by area, country, source, and topic.

Sample sites

The Embassy Page

<http://www.embpage.org> offers links to Web sites of embassies and consulates throughout the world.

One World

<http://www.oneworld.org> is "the world's biggest and best collection of multimedia material on development, the environment, and human rights on the Web."

U Languages

The WWW Virtual Library: Languages

<http://www.hardlink.com/~chambers/HLP/WWW
_Virtual_Library_Language.html> offers links to book
and text collections, multilingual resources, language labs
and institutions, and commercial resources on the Web.

Sample sites

Spiegel Online

<http://www.spiegel.de> is the online edition of the
popular German magazine.

Universal Survey of Languages

<http://www.teleport.com/~napoleon> is an ongoing
collaborative project to create a general survey of all the
world's languages.

V Law

Finding Law-Related Internet Resources

<http://www.well.com/user/cchick/sources.html> con-
tains a thorough index for all types of legal information.

Sample sites

FindLaw

<http://www.findlaw.com> is a comprehensive search
tool for legal research.

The National Law Journal

<http://www.ljextra.com/nlj> provides weekly updates
for the legal profession, including an index of the current
week's articles; full texts are available online for paid
subscribers.

W Library science

PICK

<http://www.aber.ac.uk/~tplwww/e/pick.html> is "a
gateway to quality library and information science (aka
LIS or librarianship) resources on the Internet."

Sample sites

Dewey Decimal Classification Home Page
<http://www.oclc.org/oclc/fp> is sponsored by the
OCLC Forest Press.

The Public Access Computer Systems Review
<http://info.lib.uh.edu/pacsrev.html> offers links to dis-
cussions about end-user computer systems in libraries.

x   Literature

Malaspina Great Books Home Page
<http://www.mala.bc.ca/~mcneil/template.htx> covers
links for Web resources about the Great Books series.

Internet Book Information Center
<http://sunsite.unc.edu/ibic> "represents a massive,
somewhat obsessive attempt, written primarily (but not
exclusively) by a single individual, to provide comprehensive coverage of a very wide range of issues and
interests in the field of books."

Sample sites

Alice's Adventures in Wonderland
<http://www.cs.cmu.edu/Web/People/rgs/alice
-table.html> is a hypertext version of the Lewis Carroll
story, complete with the original Tenniel illustrations.

F. Scott Fitzgerald Centenary Home Page
<http://www.sc.edu/fitzgerald> celebrates the life and
work of Fitzgerald, born in 1896.

y   Mathematics

The WWW Virtual Library: Mathematics
<http://euclid.math.fsu.edu/Science/math.html> has
links for research and education in all areas of mathe-
matics.

Sample sites

The Chance Database

<http://www.geom.umn.edu/docs/snell/chance> offers materials relevant to an introductory course in probability and statistics.

The Mathematics of Fermat's Last Theorem

<http://www.best.com/~cgd/home/flt/flt01.htm> explores the history of attempts to construct a proof for this classic theorem.

z Philosophy

The WWW Virtual Library: Philosophy

<http://www.bris.ac.uk/Depts/Philosophy/VL> offers links to resources on all aspects of philosophy and to many other detailed guides.

Sample sites

The Critical Thinking Community

<http://www.sonoma.edu/cthink>,provides a wealth of teaching and learning aids.

The University of Chicago Philosophy Project

<http://csmaclab-www.uchicago.edu/philosophy Project/philos.html> promotes the scholarly discussion of philosophical works.

aa Physics

The WWW Virtual Library: Physics

<http://www.w3.org/vl/Physics/Overview.html> categorizes physics resources by topic and by specialized field.

Sample sites

Applied Physics Letters Online

<http://www.oclc.org/oclc/menu/ejo.htm> is the elec-

tronic version of the weekly journal. (Access is limited to service subscribers.)

Fermilab: Fermi National Accelerator Laboratory

<http://www.fnal.gov> includes an online tutorial on particle physics.

JCP Express

<http://jcp.uchicago.edu> provides access to articles before they are published in the *Journal of Chemical Physics*.

bb Social sciences

Social Sciences WWW Virtual Library

<http://coombs.anu.edu.au/WWWVL-SocSci.html>, sponsored by the Australian National University, "keeps track of leading information facilities in the field of Social Sciences."

Sample sites

Impact Online

<http://www.impactonline.org> provides information about community service and activism.

The Social Psychology Network

<http://www.wesleyan.edu/psyc/psyc260>, an academic course Web page, is useful for anyone exploring psychology on the Internet.

cc Technology and applied arts

The WWW Virtual Library: Engineering

<http://arioch.gsfc.nasa.gov/wwwvl/engineering.html> offers links to resources on all aspects of engineering.

Sample sites

Architronic

<http://arcrs4.saed.kent.edu/Architronic> is a refereed electronic journal for architecture.

Science and Engineering Network News

<http://www.senn.com> is an index to engineering news; full texts are available for paid subscribers.

Index